LOCOMOTION PAPERS

The TAFF VALE LINES TO PENARTH

including the

ELY TIDAL HARBOUR AND RAILWAY
PENARTH HARBOUR, DOCK AND RAILWAY
PENARTH EXTENSION RAILWAY
CARDIFF, PENARTH AND
CADOXTON-*juxta*-BARRY JUNCTION RAILWAY

by

E. Mountford & N. Sprinks

THE OAKWOOD PRESS

ISBN 0 85361 440 7

Typeset by Gem Publishing Company, Brightwell, Wallingford, Oxfordshire.

Printed by Alpha Print (Oxon) Ltd, Witney, Oxfordshire.

Tickets courtesy of J.H. Strange Collection

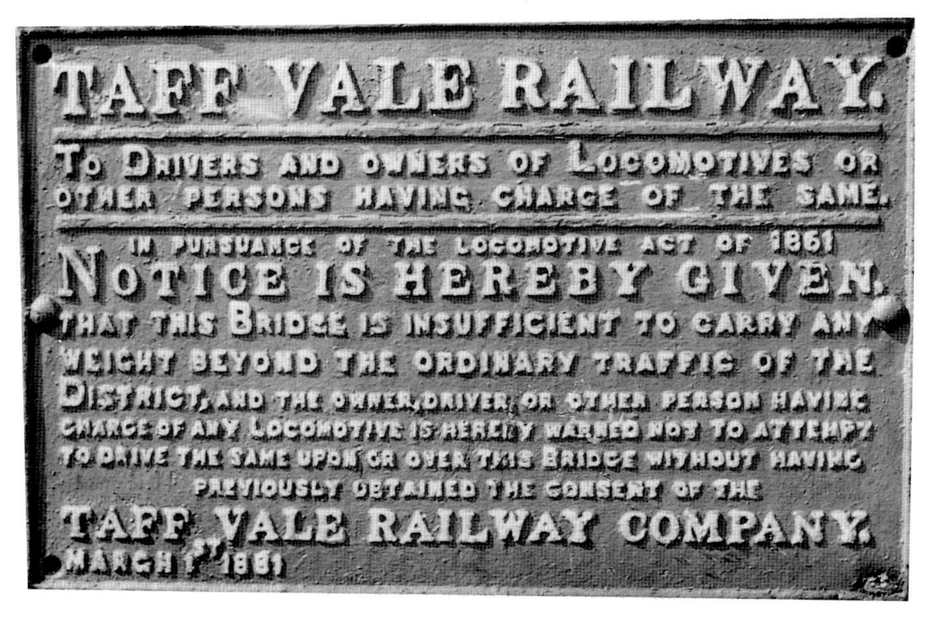

A TVR notice on a bridge over the PHDR line at Fairwater, photographed in April 1958. *R.O. Tuck*

Title page: The armorial device of the Taff Vale Railway Company.
Courtesy of The National Museum of Wales, Doctor E.S. Owen Jones' Collection

Published by
The OAKWOOD PRESS
P.O.Box 122, Headington, Oxford.

Contents

Foreword

It is a great privilege to be associated with the posthumous publication of one of the writings of Eric Mountford, who, without doubt, was one of the foremost historians of the South Wales railway scene. It was also my privilege to know Eric as a colleague in the former South Wales Divisional Headquarters of the Western Region of British Rail, and our friendship continued after each of us, in turn, took retirement from the railway service.

The text of *The Taff Vale Lines to Penarth* is largely left as Eric wrote it. It was he, after all, who had the knowledge and records, and had carried out the research. I have merely embellished the opening paragraphs, added a few facts that have come to light, principally in relation to the mid-1960s onwards, and, of course, I have had to carry on the story since Eric died in 1987. This includes the introduction of a passenger train service and stations on the northern section of the Penarth Harbour, Dock and Railway line in October 1987, after 128 years as a mainly freight carrying route: a development guaranteeing the line a special place in British railway history.

The selection of photographs has also been mine, and the individual photographers and suppliers of pictures are acknowledged in the captions. To all these people I owe my thanks, as I do to many others who have helped with the provision of information or in leading me to sources of photographs.

Dinas Powys,
South Glamorgan.
October, 1992.

Neil Sprinks

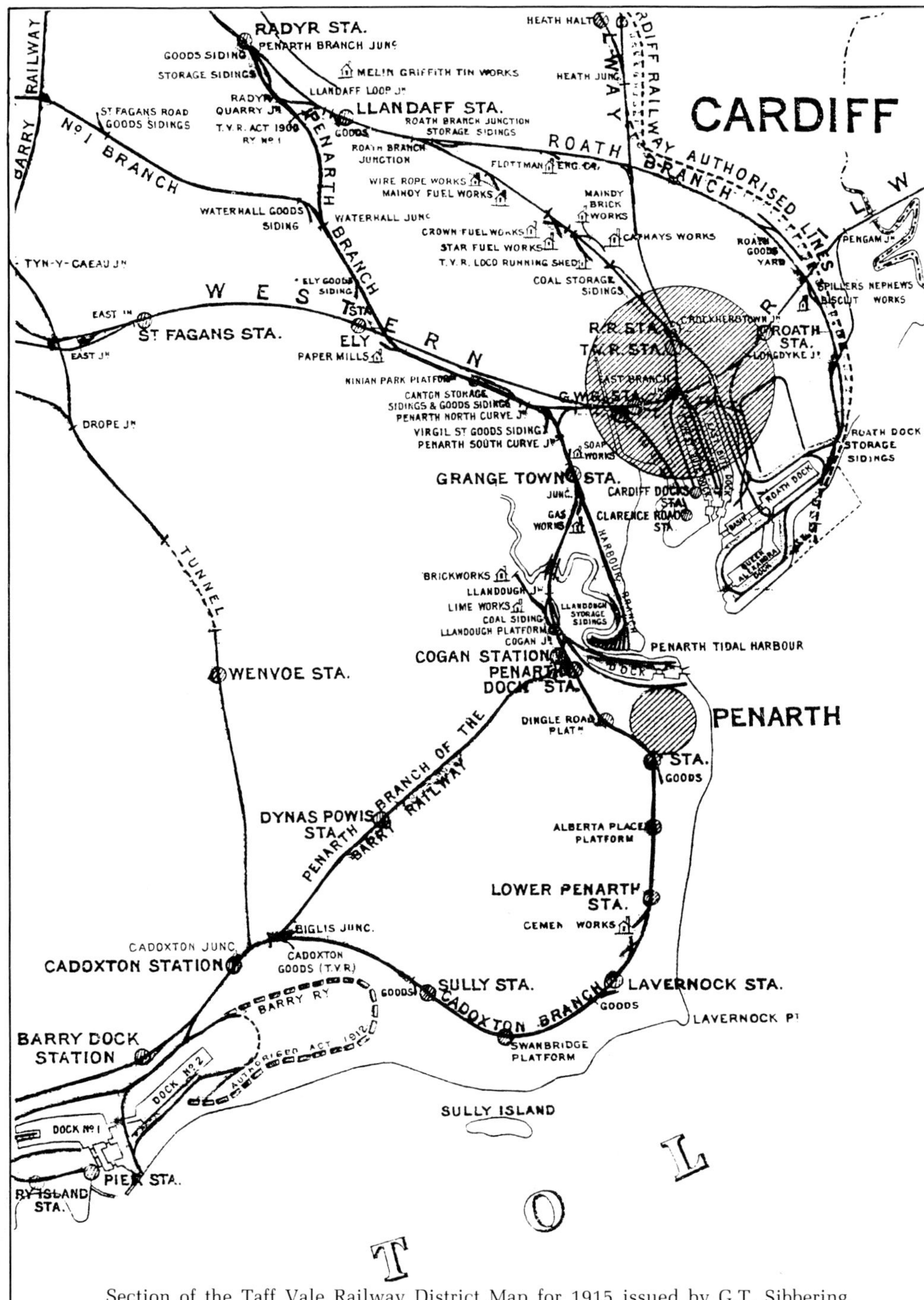

Section of the Taff Vale Railway District Map for 1915 issued by G.T. Sibbering, Engineer.

Chapter One

History and Development to 1921

The South Wales town of Penarth is today mainly residential in character and has a population of over 20,000. It lies on the estuary of the Severn south of, and across the mouths of the Ely and Taff rivers from, the Capital City of Cardiff, and owes its development to the coming of the railway: the Taff Vale Railway (TVR).

Today this railway carries a frequent service of passenger trains, but it was coal that was the driving force behind the railway's coming to Penarth and the subsequent growth of the town. Indeed, the Taff Vale Railway was bringing coal to Penarth's new dock for shipment for almost 13 years before a line was built up into the town, and passenger trains started to serve its rapidly increasing population.

A railway to Cogan Pill on the west, i.e. Penarth, bank of the river Ely was included in the original Act of Incorporation of the Taff Vale Railway in 1836. This Act, which authorised the construction of the first public railway of any real significance in Wales, provided principally for the building of the TVR's main line from Merthyr Tydfil to Cardiff, along with several branches to iron works and collieries. The movement of minerals and iron products to the sea for shipment was the prime purpose of the line, although the conveyance of passengers and general merchandise was mentioned in the Act.

The TVR was opened throughout from Merthyr Tydfil to Cardiff in 1841. Although engineered by the redoubtable Isambard Kingdom Brunel, the track gauge was the standard 4 ft 8½ in. rather than the better known broad gauge of 7 ft 0¼ in. with which he endowed the Great Western Railway and its associates – including the trunk South Wales Railway from Gloucester, through Cardiff, to Neyland.

Traffic brought down the Taff Vale Railway for shipment was taken to the then new Bute Dock in Cardiff, later known as the Bute West Dock, owned and developed by the second Marquis of Bute. Here, under an agreement of 1844, the TVR was granted a lease for the exclusive use of part of the dock: in return the TVR agreed, *inter alia*, to abandon the plan for the line to Cogan Pill, which would have involved the construction of a tidal harbour on the river Ely and therefore a diminution of the income earned by the Marquis at his dock in Cardiff. In 1848 the Marquis of Bute died, and operation of the dock was transferred to the Trustees of his Estate. In an agreement with the Trustees in 1849 the Taff Vale Railway further undertook that if it shipped traffic at any other port under its control, the same wharfage dues should be paid to the Trustees as if shipped at the Bute Dock.

It was in these circumstances that the dock situation settled down reasonably amicably until the mid-1850s. However, by that time the coal trade was increasing annually, the Rhymney Railway had been incorporated to transport and develop the mineral traffic of that valley, and the Bute Trustees were about to open their second dock, the Bute East Dock. All may still have gone smoothly but for the decided preference the Trustees were showing to the Rhymney Railway regarding the trade at the new dock, and the reluctance of the Trustees to accommodate the coal traffic from the Taff Vale at that dock.

A view south at Radyr station; when published in July 1898 in conjunction with an 'Illustrated Interview' with Ammon Beasley, the redoubtable General Manager of the Taff Vale Railway, this picture was captioned; 'Penarth Junction, where the main and Penarth Docks lines of the Taff Vale Railway converge (Radyr Passenger Station).'
Courtesy Railway Magazine

Grangetown signal box, with the lines to Ely Tidal Harbour proceeding straight ahead, and the lines to Cogan Junction and Penarth diverging to the right, photographed from the down side of Grangetown station's island platform on 5th May, 1963.
M. Hale, courtesy Great Western Trust

The freight forwarders on the TVR, with their trade developing rapidly, were alarmed at the situation, realising the Trustees were in complete command of the shipping facilities and could hold them to ransom whenever they wished. Hence in the summer of 1855 a number of the leading coal owners got together and resolved to revive the original TVR scheme of creating tidal shipping facilities on the river Ely, a mile or so south-west of the Trustees' docks. Hence later that year the promoters deposited a Bill in Parliament and, despite strong opposition from the Trustees, the Bill became law by the Ely Tidal Harbour and Railway Act dated 21st July, 1856. This authorised the construction of a tidal harbour on the eastern bank of the river Ely, along with a railway about 6¼ miles in length connecting the harbour with the Taff main line by a junction in the parish of Radyr.

The promoters, all leading men connected with the coal trade in the Taff Valleys, were the Hon. Robert Windsor Clive (owner of mineral rights), Crawshay Bailey (Aberaman), Thomas Powell (Aberdare and Llancaiach area, also Llantwit), the Rev. George Thomas (Gyfeillon), William Cartright (Llancaiach), James Insole (Rhondda Valley), Thomas Wayne (Aberdare) and John Nixon (Aberdare area). Some of the above were Directors or shareholders of the TVR but, for this scheme, acted quite independently of that company in the interests of the coal trade. In fact, although the TVR did not oppose the Bill in Parliament, other leading personalities of the 'Taff' (as the TVR was often known colloquially) spoke out about the loss of mileage on coal traffic the company would suffer by having to hand over this traffic at the junction at Radyr. However, the needs of the trade came first and the Taff sat back and awaited developments.

They did not have to wait long as the promoters, flushed with their success with the initial Bill, promptly deposited a second Bill in November 1856, seeking authority to construct a dock near the opposite bank of the Ely to the tidal harbour, and also to change the name of the company. This resulted in the Penarth Harbour Dock and Railway (PHDR) Act of 27th July, 1857 which authorised construction of the dock and a branch railway, just under two miles in length, from a junction (Grangetown Jn) with their railway authorised the previous year, crossing the river Ely and terminating at the dock. It also granted the Penarth Railway – using its short title – running powers over the whole of the TVR.

As with the 1856 Act provisions were made for working arrangements with the Taff or, subject to the approval of the shareholders of both companies, for the Taff to work the line for a period not exceeding ten years. However, by the time the railway to the tidal harbour, along with the harbour itself, was completed and opened on 4th July, 1859, no such arrangements had been made and the Penarth company purchased two mineral engines – with a third in 1860 – to work the traffic. From the records it does not appear that the Penarth company exercised their running powers over the Taff main line, contenting themselves with working the coal trains from the junction at Radyr, known as Penarth Junction, to the tidal harbour and returning the empty wagons to the junction. At the opening the harbour had 12 coal tips, but traffic at the start was not heavy, only 27,000 tons being

Ely Tidal Harbour, showing coal staithes and sailing vessels.
The National Museum of Wales

An early picture of Penarth Dock under construction. *The National Museum of Wales*

shipped in the six months of 1859, which improved to 109,000 tons during 1860.

With construction of the dock commencing as soon as the tidal harbour was opened the Taff and Penarth Directors started negotiations and a Heads of Agreement was reached in July 1862 whereby the Penarth lines were, subject to the approval of the shareholders of both companies, to be leased to the TVR for a period of 999 years. This was put to the shareholders and approved at meetings held on 12th August, 1862 and signed between the companies the following day. However, the Bute Trustees naturally objected to such a lease and applied to the Court of Chancery the same month, seeking to restrain the TVR from entering into such a lease. The Trustees failed in their action, and appealed to the House of Lords in February 1863 to reverse the verdict of the lower court, but once again the verdict went against them. As the period of the lease differed from that authorised by the 1856 and 1857 Acts the Penarth company had to obtain another Act, dated 22nd June, 1863, which authorised the 999 years. The lease for the tidal harbour and the railway from Penarth Jn to the harbour was to take effect from 1st January, 1864, the lease for the dock and railway thereto to take effect from 1st January or 1st July, whichever came first, following the public opening of the dock. The financial agreement in the lease gave the Penarth shareholders a guaranteed dividend of 4½ per cent plus half the profits from the Penarth undertaking.

Although not fully completed, Penarth Dock was opened on Saturday 10th June, 1865. Despite sailing ships far outnumbering the steam ships waiting in the Penarth Roads for the opening, it was the steam ship *William Cory* which first passed through the basin and lock into the dock. Probably it was chosen as the name was so strongly linked with the coal trade of the area. Unlike opening ceremonies these days, when the time is fixed to suit the convenience of those taking part, Penarth Dock was opened – probably due to the time of the tide – at half past seven in the morning. Nevertheless, the usual celebrities were all present and Mr James Poole, Chairman of the TVR, one of the principal speakers, stated that the Taff was one of the most successful railway undertakings in Great Britain. Success, he said, was due to their having developed the traffic *belonging* to their own railway, and not expanding right or left, eastwards or westwards, as other railways had done. He also stated that only a few years previously a London merchant had asked where Cardiff was, whereas now the answer could be given in any part of Europe, Asia, Africa or America.

However, the coal trade at Penarth did not initially expand at the rate that had been hoped. During 1864 205,000 tons of coal had been shipped at the tidal harbour, this only increased to 268,000 tons for the harbour and dock combined in 1865. Over the next few years a steady improvement was maintained and during 1870 over 900,000 tons were shipped, but the million tons per annum was not achieved until 1873 when 1,193,650 tons of coal were shipped at Penarth. After a depression in trade in 1875 when the total dipped to 1,054,000 tons, the rapid increase in the steam coal trade which followed boosted the total to over two million tons in 1881.

Before proceeding to these more prosperous days let us return to the dock as opened. Ten coaling tips were provided at the dock itself, and two more in the basin. Two tips had been removed from the tidal harbour, probably transferred to the basin, making a total of 22 tips available at Penarth. The length of the dock was 2,100 ft, and the basin 400 ft, the dock being 370 ft wide and the basin 330 ft. The total water area covered 20½ acres, of which the dock contributed 17½ acres. Vessels up to 60 feet wide could be accommodated in the dock or basin. The larger coal tips could discharge at the rate of 300 tons an hour, and the remainder, including those at the tidal harbour for the smaller vessels, at 150 tons an hour.

By their Act of 11th July, 1861 the Penarth company were empowered to make a road from the tidal harbour to the Cardiff docks area. This included a bridge over the river Taff, and for which the company exacted tolls. This bridge had a central span 60 feet wide which was opened for the passage of shipping on the river. In later years there was considerable objection to the paying of tolls for the use of the bridge and in March 1887 Cardiff Corporation paid the TVR the sum of £5,000 for the railway to lift the tolls, and at the same time commenced construction of a swing bridge as an alternative. The Corporation's Clarence Bridge opened on 17th September, 1890, and the TVR's Grangetown bridge closed in 1892 and was dismantled.

An abortive attempt to copy the Penarth undertaking was made by the first Barry Railway Company (not the later and very successful company) in 1865 and 1866. This company obtained its Act of Inauguration in 1865 and by a subsequent Act the following year, coupled with the Barry Harbour Act, also of June 1866, it was intended to construct a tidal harbour near the estuary of Barry Island, and run a railway to that harbour from the GWR South Wales main line at Peterston, seven miles west of Cardiff. By the Barry Railway (Extension) Act of 6th August, 1866 the company was empowered to construct a branch from the authorised railway, at Cadoxton, to join the Penarth Railway at Cogan. If proceeded with this would have entailed a broad gauge railway from Cadoxton to Peterston, a standard gauge branch to Cogan, and a mixed gauge line from Cadoxton to the harbour at Barry. However the company received little support from the traders and the scheme was abandoned.

At the same time the GWR were taking an interest in the Penarth line in connection with their coal traffic from the Ogmore and Ely valleys. In the initial Ely Tidal Harbour Act of 1856, and again in the Penarth Dock Act of the following year, provision had been made for a junction with the South Wales Railway (SWR) where the two railways ran parallel between Ely station (SWR) and Canton (Cardiff), and mixed gauge would have been laid between that junction and the dock and harbour at Penarth.

Hence, in connection with the Ogmore Valley Railway Bill, the GWR obtained a Further Powers Act on 30th July, 1866 which contained provision for two connections with the Penarth Railway west of Cardiff, the first a link 54 chains in length connecting southwards with the Penarth Railway, the other 38 chains long making a northwards connection. With the failure of the Ogmore scheme the GWR made no move to construct these connections, but did not allow the time limit to expire and obtained an extension by their 1869 Act. By their Additional Powers Act of 31st July, 1871 the GWR abandoned the second connection authorised by the 1866 Act and substituted an alternative northern connection 22 chains in length, commencing by a junction with the first link and terminating by a junction with the Penarth line in a northerly direction. Thus the triangle of lines which still exist adjacent to Canton sheds was created. Following the conversion of their South Wales lines from broad to standard gauge in May 1872, the GWR commenced constructing the two loop connections, but these were not completed and opened until December 1875. The loop authorised in 1866 is known as Penarth Curve East, and the 1871 loop as Penarth Curve North. By an agreement dated 24th April, 1866 the TVR obtained running powers over the east curve, which thus gave them continuous running powers from their main line from South Wales Junction, immediately south of the Taff's Cardiff (now Queen Street) station, to Penarth harbour, or dock, via the GWR (now Central) station. This started prolonged negotiations, often of a strained character, between the two companies regarding allowing Taff trains to use the GWR station. At one stage there was talk of rebuilding the GWR station as a joint station, but the terms were too harsh for the Taff to accept, and the GWR built a completely new station on their own, on the original site, in 1876 and 1877. Having to foot the bill themselves, they were determined to keep the Taff out of the station as far as they could, but that is a later story and we must return to developments at the dock.

Until 1864 all coal shipments at the tidal harbour had originated from traders on the Taff Vale line, but during that year the Rhymney Railway, which at that time was using the Taff main line between Walnut Tree Jn (Taffs Well) and Crockherbtown Jn (Cardiff) *en route* to the Bute East Dock, started depositing a few of their coal trains at Penarth Jn (Radyr) for shipment at Penarth. This traffic was comparatively light initially, 14,671 tons in 1864 and 16,838 tons the following year, but in 1866 it almost doubled to 31,578 tons. The TVR traffic created no problems, following the lease of the Penarth undertaking to the Taff, the latter's engines working the trains directly from the colliery to the dock or harbour. A different situation arose with the Rhymney valley coal, as the Rhymney Railway (RR) had no running powers over the Penarth line which meant that TVR engines had to be available at the junction to take the trains onwards. For the first couple of years of the RR working this presented no great difficulty, but with the traffic increasing it became necessary, in 1866, to lay down storage sidings immediately south of the junction at Radyr, together with an engine shed for the Taff engines working between the junction and the dock. The Rhymney traffic developed steadily and during 1869 129,286 tons of coal were left at Penarth Jn, which had further increased to 229,650 tons during 1873. However, this traffic fluctuated according to the available capacity at Cardiff Docks, reaching 319,641 tons in 1885 only to fall to 189,313 tons in 1887 following the opening of the Roath Dock at Cardiff.

The opening of the dock at Penarth increased the hostility between the Taff and the Bute Trustees. Despite losing their legal battle to try to prevent

A down coal train arriving at Radyr in 1923, hauled by ex-TVR 'K' class 0–6–0 No. 1001 (TVR No. 359). The passenger station can be seen alongside.
Courtesy Great Western Trust

A view of Penarth Dock, *circa* 1883. *B.J. Miller Collection*

the Taff taking over the lease of the Penarth undertaking, the Trustees determined to demand the dock dues to which they felt they were entitled under the terms of their 1849 lease of the Bute West Dock to the Taff. This was that the TVR should ship all their coal at the Bute dock, and should any be shipped by them elsewhere, the same dock dues should be received by the Trustees as if such coal were shipped at the Bute dock. Initially the Trustees demanded such dock dues for all traffic passing over the TVR for shipment at Penarth and, on this being refused, sought legal redress by bringing an action in the Court of Queens Bench on 29th April, 1870. The Taff argued that the Penarth undertaking was not part of the TVR, also that some of their coal traffic was similarly handed over to another company and shipped elsewhere – they quoted coal passed to the GWR at Quakers Yard and eventually shipped at Birkenhead. On this basis the Court found in favour of the TVR, which was upheld on appeal to the House of Lords on 23rd May, 1871.

This was not the end of the matter as the Bute Trustees put in a very similar claim to the Court of Exchequer Chamber on 16th June, 1871, and that court upheld the claim. If that verdict had not been challenged the future of Penarth as a port would have been seriously in doubt. On this occasion, it was the Taff that took the matter on appeal to the House of Lords where, after a postponement in the 1872 Session, the case was eventually heard before Lord Cairns, Lord Chelmsford and Lord Colonsay on 21st and 28th April, 1873. Their verdict was in favour of the Taff, but Lord Cairns made it quite clear that the Taff had succeeded purely on a technical point. The decision clearly rested on the point of whether the Penarth undertaking could be taken as part of the TVR company or not. They reluctantly came to the conclusion that although the Taff held the lease of the Penarth company, the latter had been authorised by Parliament as a separate company, and unless amalgamated with the Taff, remained a separate company. In his judgement, delivered early in May 1873, Lord Cairns said:

> I cannot help feeling some regret at the result at which I am obliged to arrive . . . the TVR company have departed in a clear and striking manner from the good faith of the arrangement which was made, by the lease and the covenants contained therein, but have kept themselves from the obligation of the letter of the covenants.

Thus the fate of Penarth Dock and Harbour was decided, it had been a very near thing and, if the decision had gone the other way and the Taff had had to pay dues on all shipments made at Penarth, then the latter could hardly have survived. There is no doubt the Trustees contributed to their own downfall by their decided preference to the Rhymney Railway as, but for that, it is extremely doubtful if the Penarth scheme would ever have arisen.

The rapid increase in the steam coal trade in the late 1860s and early 1870s led to an extension of Penarth Dock. One clause in the agreement made between the Trustees of Lord Windsor and the Penarth company was that the dock must be enlarged when the average tonnage of coal shipped exceeded 50,000 tons per acre during three consecutive years. As the acreage of the dock and basin at that time was twenty and a half, this meant that when over 1,025,000 tons was recorded during three consecutive years, an

The ex-Taff Vale Railway signal box at Waterhall Junction, complete with somersault signal, photographed on 12th July, 1952. The photographer is facing Radyr, with the 'Llantrisant No. 1 Railway' to Common Branch Junction diverging to the left.
R.C. Riley

A view of Radyr Quarry in 1884, with a TVR 0–6–0 'L' class locomotive on stone wagons. The quarry was alongside the PHDR line south of Penarth Junction (Radyr) and gave its name to Radyr Quarry Junction and signal box, a TVR signal box still standing (1992) at this point, and in use. *The National Museum of Wales*

extension was to be undertaken. This was achieved during the years 1872–4 when the totals of 941,222 tons, 1,193,650 tons and 1,137,023 tons gave an average of 1,090,631 tons per annum for the three years. However 1875 proved to be a very bleak year for trade in east South Wales, the miners were on strike for a very lengthy spell from the beginning of the year, resulting in the complete closure of some ironworks as well as collieries. This had its reaction in the trade figures for the next two or three years, and it was not until late 1880 that the Penarth company put forward a Bill to sanction extension to the dock. This received the Royal Assent on 3rd June, 1881, and the TVR issued contracts for the work to commence immediately.

This Act also contained a clause confirming an agreement made between the Penarth company and Lord Windsor that:

> Within two years from the passing of this Act the Penarth company, or the Taff Vale company, shall construct and for ever thereafter keep open, a passenger station at the Penarth Junction, at Radyr.

Radyr station was opened on 1st June, 1883 just two days within the time limit and is still open today. Although the station, sited on the Taff main line just nine chains north of the junction, was named Radyr, the Taff preferred the name Penarth Jn for both the junction and the engine shed, and only changed the name for these two to Radyr shortly after World War I.

Following the 1881 Act the north end of Penarth Dock was extended for a length of 270 yds, this extension being officially opened on 9th April, 1884. At that time the complete length of the dock was given as 2,900 ft, and the area of dock and basin as 26½ acres. By that time there were 16 tips in use at the dock and basin and these, in much later days, were renewed to deal with 20 ton wagons. Despite the fierce competition from other railways and docks from the 1880s onwards, the steam coal trade expanded at such a rate that coal exports from Penarth Dock and Harbour reached a peak of 4,513,117 tons in 1913. About that time it was said that the tonnage exported per acre of dock space per annum was greater at Penarth than at any other port in the world.

Two railway junctions were made with the Penarth line as the steam coal trade grew to its peak, but neither had much bearing on the traffic to Penarth or its dock. The first was a TVR branch from Common Branch Junction (north of Cross Inn, on the Llantrisant–Pontypridd line) to Waterhall Junction on the Penarth line, sited a short distance northwards from the present day Fairwater station. This branch, opened on 11th September, 1886, was intended as a 'short cut' route for coal traffic from the Ely and Treferig Valleys to Penarth Docks. However the Ely coal was generally speaking, all taken by the GW route via Llantrisant, whilst the Treferig coal never amounted to much and was finally worked out in 1904. This branch, always referred to as Llantrisant No. 1 Railway, became something of a white elephant afterwards despite some quarry traffic; even so the Taff made use of it – a convenient quiet branch – to trial their new engines and those that had received heavy repairs at the Taff's locomotive shops at West Yard Cardiff Docks. No. 1 Steam Rail Car is known to have undergone her initial trials over the branch late in 1903, while a Sunday School excursion from Llant-

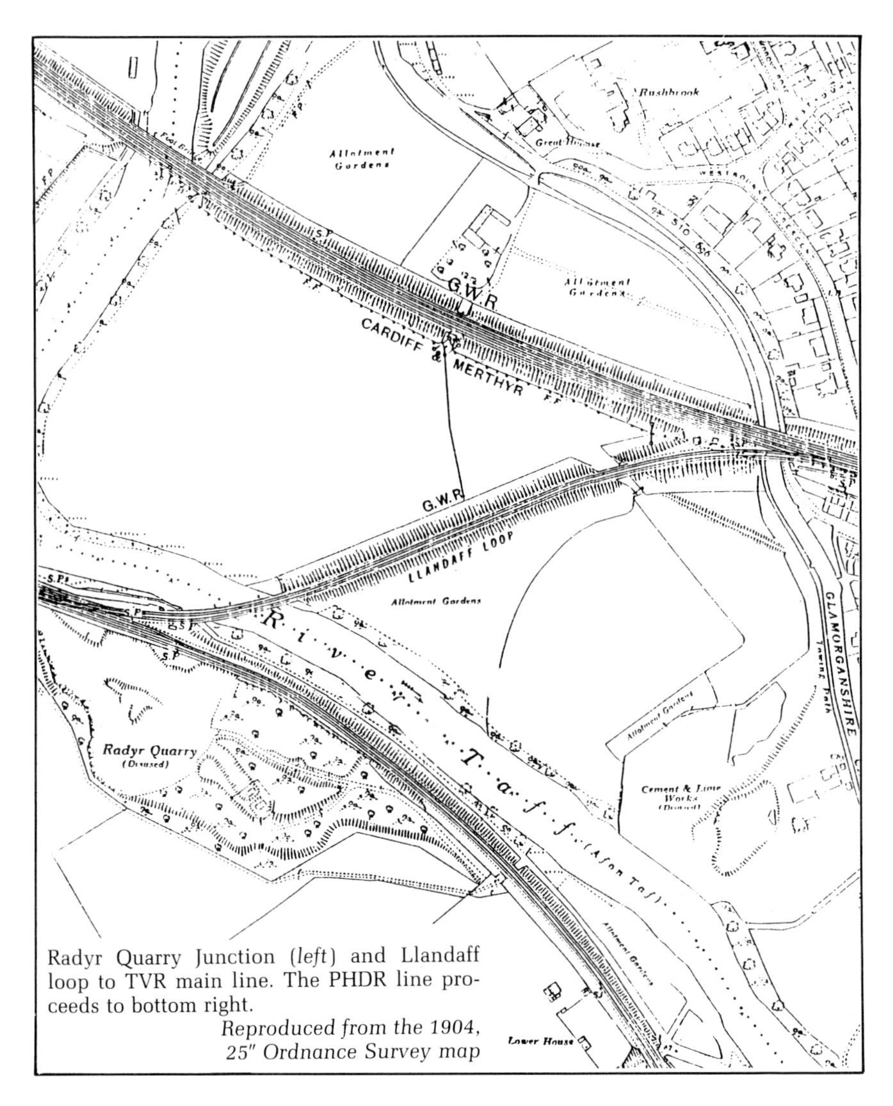

Radyr Quarry Junction (*left*) and Llandaff loop to TVR main line. The PHDR line proceeds to bottom right.

Reproduced from the 1904, 25" Ordnance Survey map

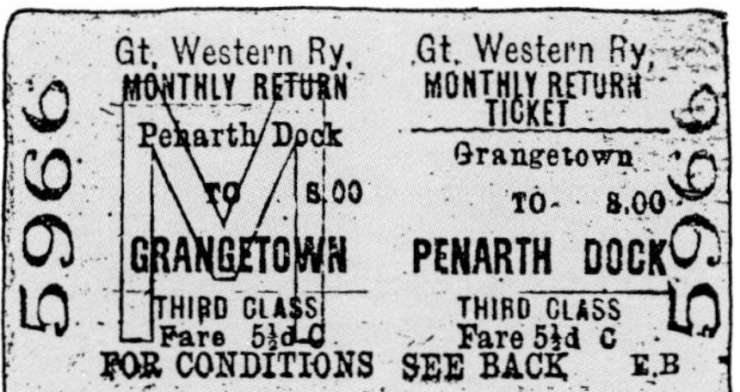

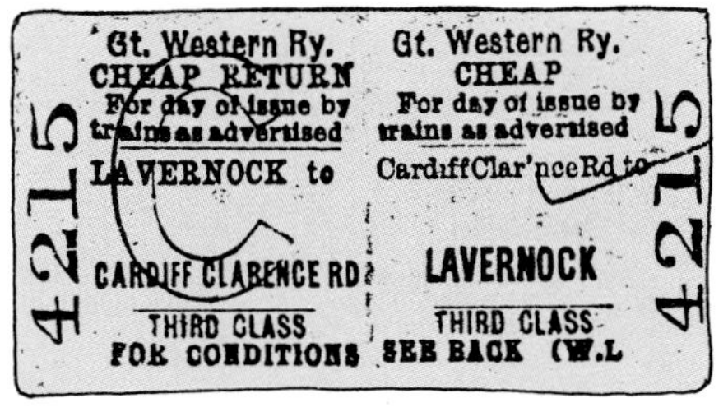

wit Fardre to Penarth in the early 1910s is reputed to have been routed this way. (The Waterhall Junction end of the line was to close on 28th September, 1964.)

The other branch, known as the Llandaff Loop, was a mere 29 chains long, a connecting loop from the south end of Radyr yard, at Radyr Quarry Junction on the Penarth line, back into the TVR main line at Llandaff. This opened on 28th May, 1900 to allow coal traffic and empties passing through Radyr Yard to make a southern connection with the main line, or to pass on to the Roath branch if required. The loop still exists (although it was singled as from 4th July, 1966).

With the rapidly increasing steam coal trade in the last decade of the 19th century the Taff, under the guise of separate companies, promoted three successive Bills in a vain attempt to construct another dock in the vicinity of the Tidal Harbour. The first Bill, promoted in the 1896 Session, was called the Windsor Dock Bill. This sought authorisation for the construction of a dock on the mud flats immediately east of the estuary of the River Ely. If this scheme had been successful a large area of the flats under water at high tide, would have had to be reclaimed and protected by an embankment built into the Bristol Channel. The dock would have covered 29 acres with an entrance lock covering a further 1½ acres. However the opposition from other local dock interests secured the rejection of the Bill. The following session a very similar Bill was promoted, with a slightly smaller proposed dock of 26½ acres, and an entrance lock covering 2 acres. The site was almost as the first Bill and, once again, the opposition was too powerful and the Bill rejected.

The Taff management decided to fight yet again, and instructed their Engineer to produce an entirely fresh scheme for the 1898 Session. On that occasion a much larger dock of 42 acres was proposed, this sited well away from the seashore, almost alongside the existing tidal harbour. At this point the River Ely flows in a succession of horseshoe bends, and it would have been necessary to take out one bend completely and replace it by a straight cut. (In this connection Brunel's original intention in 1835–6 was to make a straight cut at the same point, but the straight cut would have been left as a tidal harbour.) The proposed dock of 1898 required an entrance dock of 2½ acres and this would have completely cut across the existing branch to the harbour, hence it appears that the tidal harbour would have been abandoned and its trade incorporated in the new dock.

Once again the Bill failed, and on that occasion the Taff accepted defeat and the Windsor Dock schemes were consigned to the archives. In 1901 in an effort to do something at Penarth, the Taff installed four new improved coal tipping appliances at the Basin, and several instances of very quick loading were afterwards recorded. One steamer loaded 2,115 tons of coal, plus bunkering, in one hour and fifty seven minutes, arriving and departing on the same tide, whilst another loaded over 4,000 tons in three hours and forty minutes. Such was the steam coal trade from the South Wales ports in the early years of the present century. Before leaving the proposed Windsor Dock schemes it should be mentioned that rail access, in each case, would have been by the Penarth Harbour branch, which would certainly have had to be increased from two to four lines, if any of the schemes had been successful.

A postcard reflecting the early municipal expansion of Penarth, showing churches, public library, pier and shopping centre. *Lens of Sutton*

Another early postcard showing the first development of Penarth's esplanade and pier. *Lens of Sutton*

Activity in Penarth Dock, 1897. *The National Museum of Wales*

A period picture of the down side forecourt of Penarth Town station, facing Plymouth Road, with the station building on the left and the public house beyond. *Lens of Sutton*

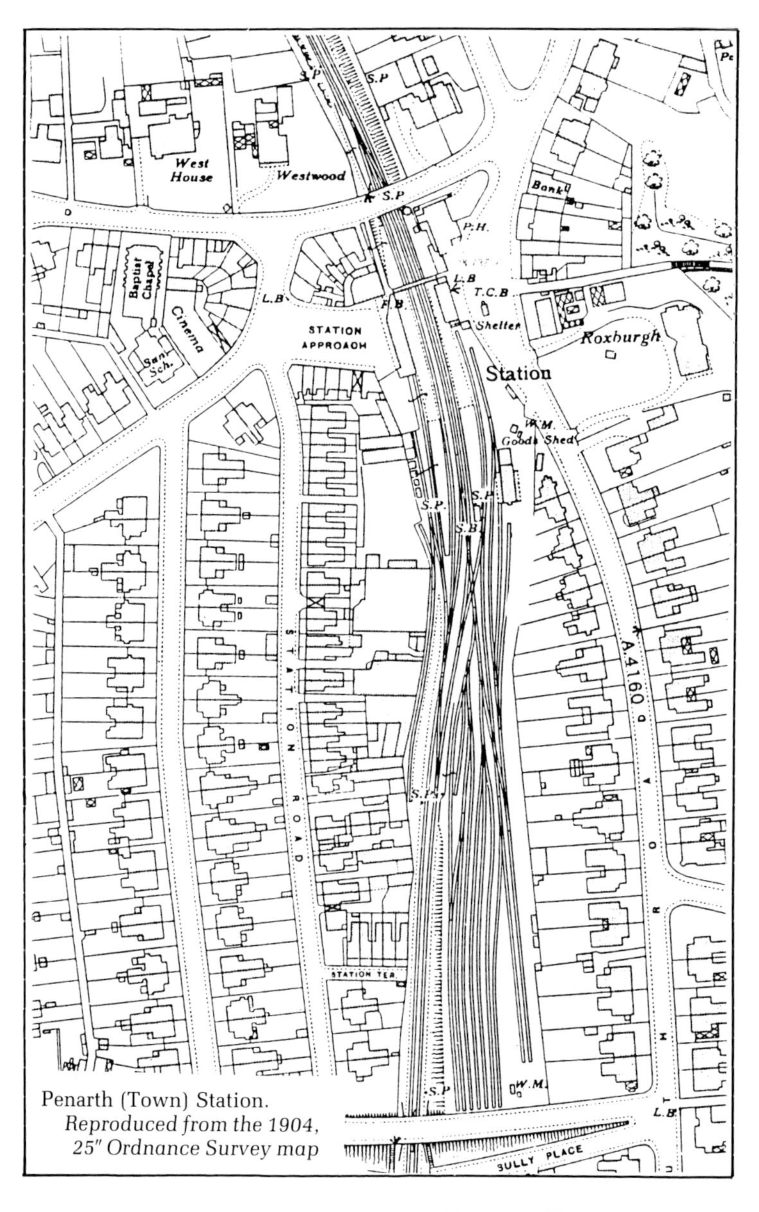

Penarth (Town) Station.
Reproduced from the 1904, 25" Ordnance Survey map

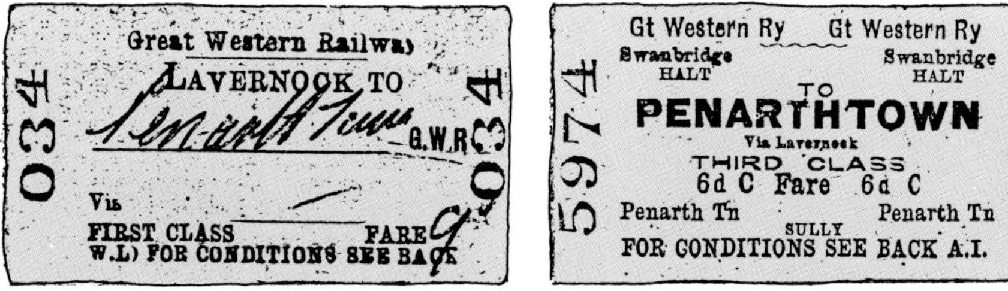

Meanwhile, moving over to passenger traffic, following the opening of Penarth Curve East by the GWR in 1875, there was renewed demand for passenger communication between Penarth and Cardiff. When the Penarth railway was in its infancy in 1861 the population of Penarth was only 1,406, and this had only increased to 1,882 by 1870. On 5th January of that year the Taff opened the Penarth Hotel for the convenience of traders, although in 1879 they leased the hotel to the proprietor of the Royal Hotel, Cardiff (the hotel building in Penarth is now Headlands School). By the mid-1870s Penarth's population had increased to around 3,500, but would have grown far more rapidly if there had been a rail passenger service to Cardiff. Penarth itself was (and still is) a very pleasant place to live, the housing springing up near the seashore, that area being hidden from the docks by Penarth Head.

Hence in 1875 a company called the Penarth, Sully and Cadoxton Railway promoted a Bill to construct a coastal line, commencing by a junction with the Penarth Railway at Cogan, climbing up the hillside to the west of Penarth Dock to Penarth Town, and thence along the coast to Sully where the railway would curve inland to Cadoxton. Running powers were sought over the Penarth Railway to Penarth Curve and thence over the GWR into their Cardiff station. In this form the Bill received little support, particularly from the TVR who saw it as a white elephant west of Penarth. Hence, during its parliamentary progress, it was modified accordingly and received the Royal Assent as the Penarth Extension Railway (PER) Act of 11th August, 1876. This authorised the railway one mile and ten chains in length, from a junction with the Penarth Railway at Cogan, near Penarth Dock, to Penarth Town. Clause 26 provided that either the TVR or GWR or both jointly, should work and manage the line. The Taff immediately took up this option and by agreement dated 17th August, 1876, confirmed by a later agreement dated 27th September, 1877, consented to work the line for a period of 99 years.

From the date of the first agreement the Taff completely controlled the PER, and paid the full cost of a station erected near Cogan Pill (Penarth Dock). They also negotiated with the GWR as to charges for the use of the latter's Cardiff station, and the running powers from Penarth Curve South Jn to that station. Although these charges were considered quite excessive by the Taff, they were reluctantly agreed to, and TVR records state that the line to Penarth Town opened on 1st January, 1878. If so, this must have been for a small amount of goods or parcel traffic as, a few days later Colonel Rich, inspecting on behalf of the Board of Trade, requested some minor signalling improvements before passengers were carried. His recommendations were quickly carried out and on his second inspection, on 14th February, the Colonel declared all was well, and the long awaited passenger service between Penarth and Cardiff (GWR station) commenced on Wednesday 20th February, 1878.

The initial service was eight trains in each direction, with all three classes catered for, on weekdays only, no Sunday service being provided. The journey, including the stop at Penarth Dock station, occupied 15 minutes in either direction. During the first week 3,952 people paid to travel on the trains, and this was considered reasonable, as the population of Penarth was

An up train in Penarth Dock station in 1905, with Penarth Dock behind. The locomotive is recorded as '0.2' Class 0–6–2T No. 83. To the left is the River Ely; Ely Tidal Harbour, on the left bank, is out of view. *National Museum of Wales, Spencer Powell Collection*

only about the same figure at that time. In Cardiff, the TVR had hoped to have its own booking office for the trains in Penarth Road, at the rear of the GWR station, but the latter company refused to agree and insisted that they should issue the tickets from their existing booking office. One further station, Grangetown – then two separate words – first appeared in Bradshaw's timetable in December 1882, but probably opened a month or two earlier. This was sited at the junction of the harbour branch with the lines to Penarth and the dock. No further stations were ever opened between Penarth and Cardiff, although in the early years of the present century a couple of rail motor halts were added, which will be described later in this chapter.

Having achieved passenger communication between Penarth and Cardiff the Taff's next objective was, naturally, to set up through running between their own main line (at the present day Queen Street station) and Penarth via the GWR station. This was fiercely resisted by the GWR as such trains then had to cross the GWR South Wales main line on the level at the east end of the GWR station, and it was not until 19th December, 1881 that passengers were allowed into the GWR station over the link from the TVR (now Queen Street) station. These were purely inter-station locals and through running between the Taff main line and Penarth Town was not achieved until Thursday 1st February, 1883, following agreement reached between the two companies the previous day. This allowed certain TVR main line trains to and from Cardiff Docks (now Bute Road) station to be re-routed at the TVR Cardiff station to run to and from Penarth Town via the GWR Cardiff station and Penarth Curve East.

To enable passenger tank engines to turn, a 30 ft turntable had been installed at Penarth Town together with watering facilities, an engine pit, and carriage sidings. But it soon became necessary to stable passenger engines at Penarth and this, in addition to the need to stable some mineral engines and dock shunters at Penarth, led to a three road engine shed being erected alongside Penarth Dock station in 1887.

Whilst the original Penarth lines, both to the harbour and the dock, had been laid double track at the start, the mainly passenger Penarth Extension line was single, and not doubled until 1893. Despite this, a second platform had been added to Penarth Town station as from 15th April, 1889. The harbour line remained double track throughout, but the vast increase in the coal trade caused a third line to be added between Penarth Curve South and Llandough (between Grangetown and Cogan Jn) in 1885, extensive coal storage sidings being laid at Llandough for the Penarth Dock traffic. This third line was extended to Cogan Jn in 1891, and a few years later the line between Penarth Curve and Cogan Jn was quadrupled, but more of that later.

Despite the PHDR and PER being completely worked and managed by the TVR, both companies remained nominally independent until the main grouping of railways in Great Britain in 1922–3. Without doubt, as far as the PHDR was concerned, this was due to the legal action of the Bute Trustees which ended in 1873, otherwise the Penarth companies would almost certainly have been amalgamated with the Taff in 1889, as most of the other concerns it managed were. If the Penarth company had been included it appears that the Bute interests could once again have taken legal action

A view of Llandough sidings, looking towards Cardiff, in the late 1880s. An 'L' class 0–6–0 stands on the down line, while the locomotive shunting in the sidings is thought to be one of the 0–6–0Ts purchased from the Metropolitan Railway.

Courtesy Great Western Trust

A newly built bridge on the CPBJR line, with a contractor's locomotive visible. This bridge is thought to be that carrying the railway over the then new Dinas Powys to Barry road. *The National Museum of Wales*

against the Taff, and with a reasonably good chance of success. The PHDR was absorbed into the GWR – along with the TVR – by the Preliminary Absorption Scheme No. 1 dated 9th May, 1922, backdated to 1st January, 1922 for accountancy purposes. The Penarth Extension Railway remained nominally independent until the following year, being absorbed as from 1st January, 1923 by Scheme No. 3 dated 19th January, 1923.

Returning to the dock trade and the extension of Penarth Dock in 1884, by that time both the Bute Trustees and the TVR were facing the most serious threat to their trade that had arisen up to that time. A second breakaway group of coal freighters had got together and formed the Barry Dock and Railway, and that company had obtained Parliamentary authorisation to extract traffic from the collieries served by the Taff, at both Trehafod and Treforest. Whilst the main threat of the Barry company does not form part of the story of the Penarth lines, it did have considerable repercussions in that area. Immediately following the passing of the Barry company's Act of Incorporation in August 1884, the Taff promoted a satellite company, the Cardiff, Penarth and Cadoxton-*juxta*-Barry Jn Railway (CPBJR) in a vain effort to:

a) prevent any expansion of the authorised Barry Dock,
b) prevent any extension of the Barry Railway towards Cardiff, or Penarth,
c) connect the Penarth lines with the authorised Barry Railway at Cadoxton – almost at the gates of Barry Dock – and thus attempt to hand over the coal traffic at that point in lieu of at Trehafod or Treforest, as authorised by the Barry Act.

A Bill, accompanied by plans of the proposed CPBJR, was deposited in November 1884, six short railways being included:

1) A direct railway 3 m. 23 ch. in length from a junction with the Penarth line near Cogan Pill to approaching the authorised Barry Ry at Cadoxton.
2) A short connecting line 30½ ch. in length from the termination of Railway No. 1 to the Barry line.
3) A coastal railway 3 m. 78 ch. in length from the termination of the Penarth Extension Railway at Penarth Town to Sully.
4) A short connecting line 1 m. 1½ ch. in length from the termination of Railway 3 to connect with the (head-on) junction of Railways Nos. 1 & 2 near Cadoxton.
5) A railway 3 m. 22 ch. in length from the termination of Railway 3 at Sully to Barry.
6) A short branch, 30½ ch. long, from the Penarth Railway, north of the bridge over the river Ely to Grange Town Iron Works.

Railways 1 & 2, the direct line from Cogan to Cadoxton, were intended to forestall any Barry ambition to get to Cardiff and, at the same time, create a convenient route by which coal originating on the Taff system, could be handed over to the Barry Railway well within a mile of the latter's authorised dock. Railway 5 would have crossed westwards from Sully towards Barry Dock, thus preventing any extension of that dock. Near the authorised dock, the proposed railway would have veered northwards and passed over the Barry Railway, and then westwards to run almost parallel to it, with its terminus near the west end of the present Barry station.

The Barry countered the Taff Bill by depositing one of their own, seeking construction of a railway from Cadoxton to Cogan 3 m. 57 ch. in length,

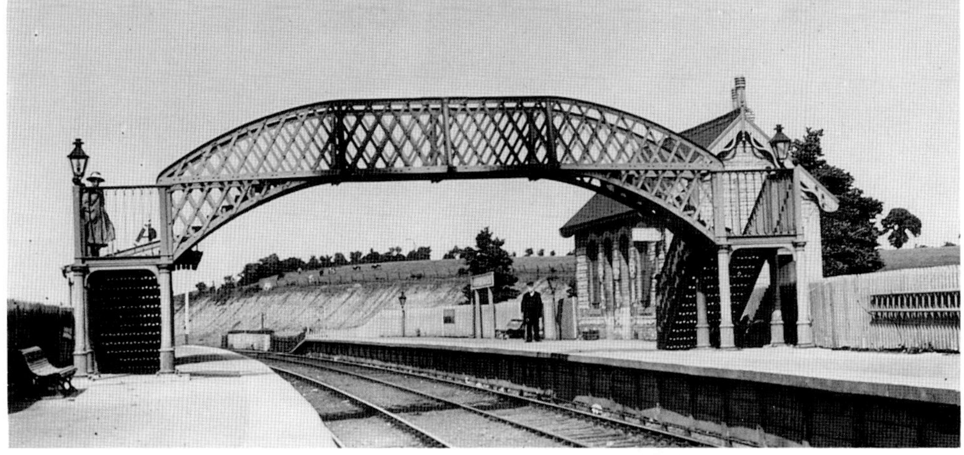

Lavernock station, looking towards Penarth, in June 1921.
B.J. Miller Collection

A close-up view of ironwork and TVR lamp on footbridge at Lavernock station. *I.L. Wright*

A roof bracket at Sully station incorporating the CPBJ initials of the Cardiff, Penarth and (Cadoxton-*juxta-*) Barry Junction Railway, photographed in April 1958. *I.L. Wright*

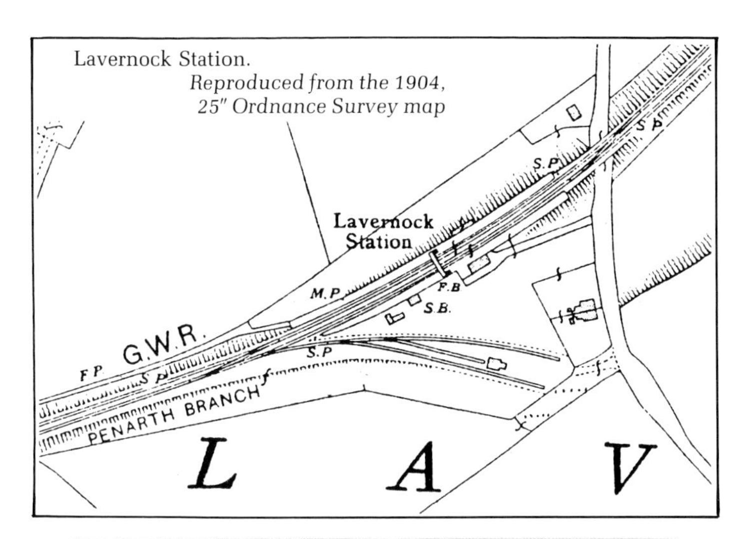

Lavernock Station.
Reproduced from the 1904, 25" Ordnance Survey map

A detailed view of the lamp on footbridge at Lavernock station. *I.L. Wright*

An early picture of Sully station and goods yard, looking towards Penarth.
Courtesy Great Western Trust

A busy scene at Sully station in TVR days, with an up train at the platform.
Lens of Sutton

almost identical to Railways 1 and 2 of the CPBJR proposals. The Barry won the day and by their Act of 31st July, 1885 obtained authorisation to construct the Cadoxton to Cogan line. Besides rejecting the CPBJR's proposals for that line, they also rejected Railway No. 5, leaving that company – by their Act of 6th August, 1885 – only powers to construct the coastal railway to Sully and thence to connect with the Barry Railway at Biglis Jn, 32 chains east of Cadoxton. The Act also authorised the branch to Grange Town ironworks, although this was never constructed, the works being almost alongside the Penarth Harbour branch, and better served from that branch. Thus the Taff were left with authority to construct some five miles of coastal railway, through sparsely populated countryside, over which little traffic could ever be expected.

Nevertheless construction commenced without delay and the first section, from Penarth Town to a station at Lavernock, some 1¾ miles, was opened for passenger traffic on 1st December, 1887. The day prior to this opening the CPBJR deposited a further Bill, for the 1888 Session, once again seeking authority to construct a branch railway that would effectively prevent expansion of Barry Dock, by that time well under construction. The proposed branch was once again from a junction with the authorised line at Sully, terminating near the east end of Barry Dock, with a short road from that terminus to the existing road from Cardiff to Barry. The proposed branch was 1 m. 50½ ch. in length. However, the Bill was rejected as the Parliamentary committee was not impressed that this branch railway was either necessary or to the public's advantage, hence once again the Taff's ambition to prevent any expansion of Barry Dock was thwarted.

The CPBJR was completed to the junction with the Barry line in November 1888 and approved by Colonel Rich on behalf of the BoT on the 30th of that month. The Taff intimated to the Barry that they intended to extend their passenger service from Lavernock into the Barry's Cadoxton station as from 3rd December. (At that date the Barry Co. had not even opened their railway, although a passenger service between Barry Dock and Cogan did open on 20th December.) Hence on Monday 3rd December the Taff presented their train, with 10 passengers booked through to Cadoxton, at Biglis Junction, but were unable to get on to Barry Railway metals, as a line of contractor's wagons had been conveniently placed across the junction. At the signal box there were only Saxby and Farmer's men (signalling contractors) in attendance, so the Taff train had to withdraw.

For the time being the passenger service still had to terminate at Lavernock, although the goods station at Sully had been opened for traffic since 5th November, 1888. The passenger services were extended to that station on Monday 24th December. In view of the Barry's continued refusal to let the Taff trains into Cadoxton, the Taff secured some land immediately on their own side of the junction and erected a temporary station there called Biglis Jn, to which the passenger service from Penarth was extended on 8th July, 1889.

The Barry Co. sat back and awaited developments. So far – despite Parliamentary authority – they had prevented Taff trains coming upon their line, and they knew the Biglis station was little more than a white elephant.

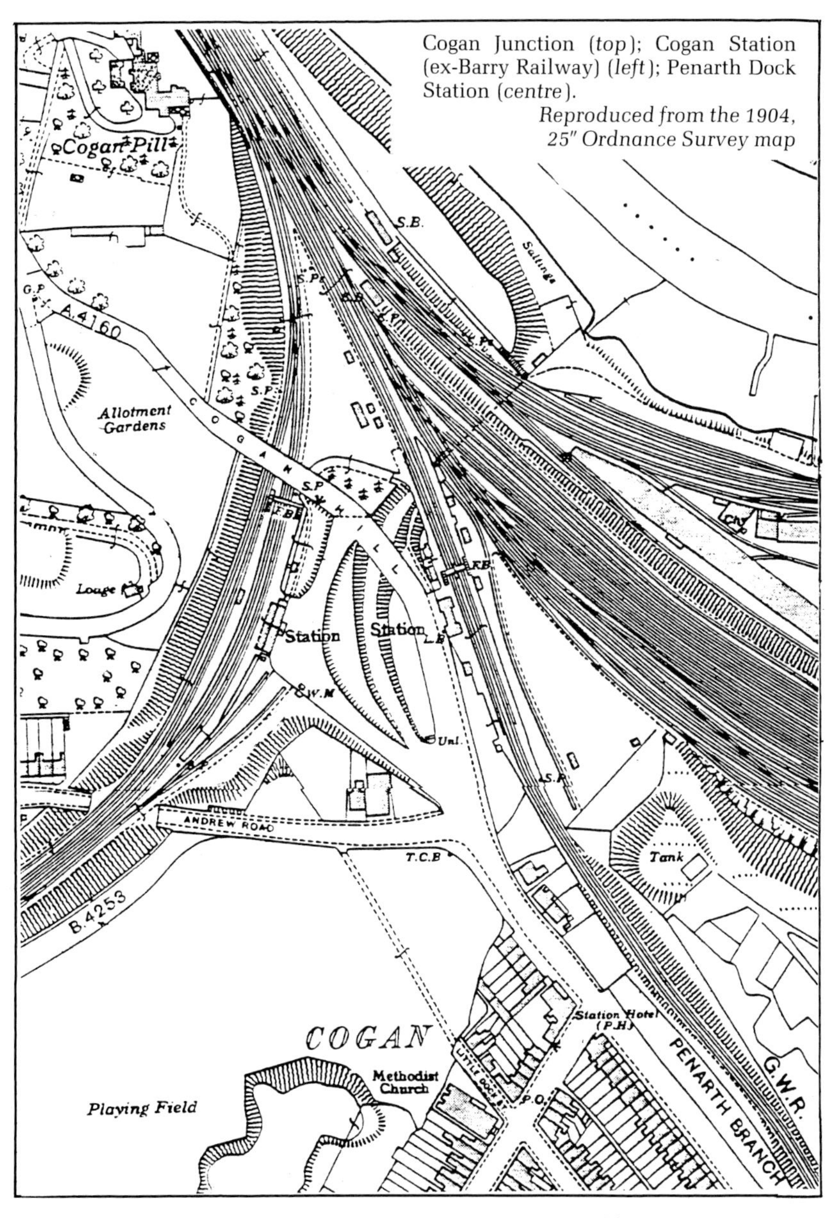

Cogan Junction (*top*); Cogan Station (ex-Barry Railway) (*left*); Penarth Dock Station (*centre*).

Reproduced from the 1904, 25″ Ordnance Survey map

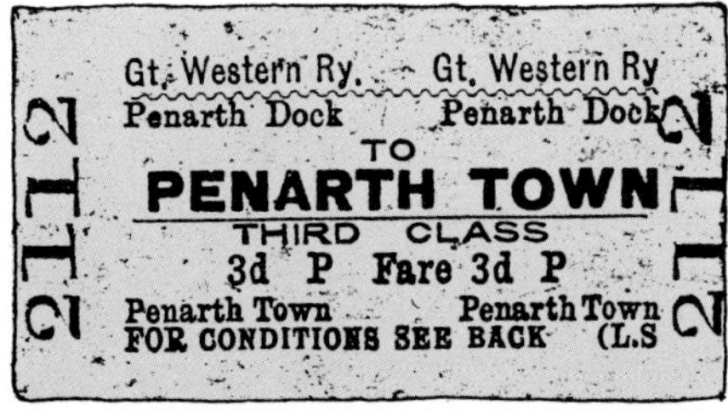

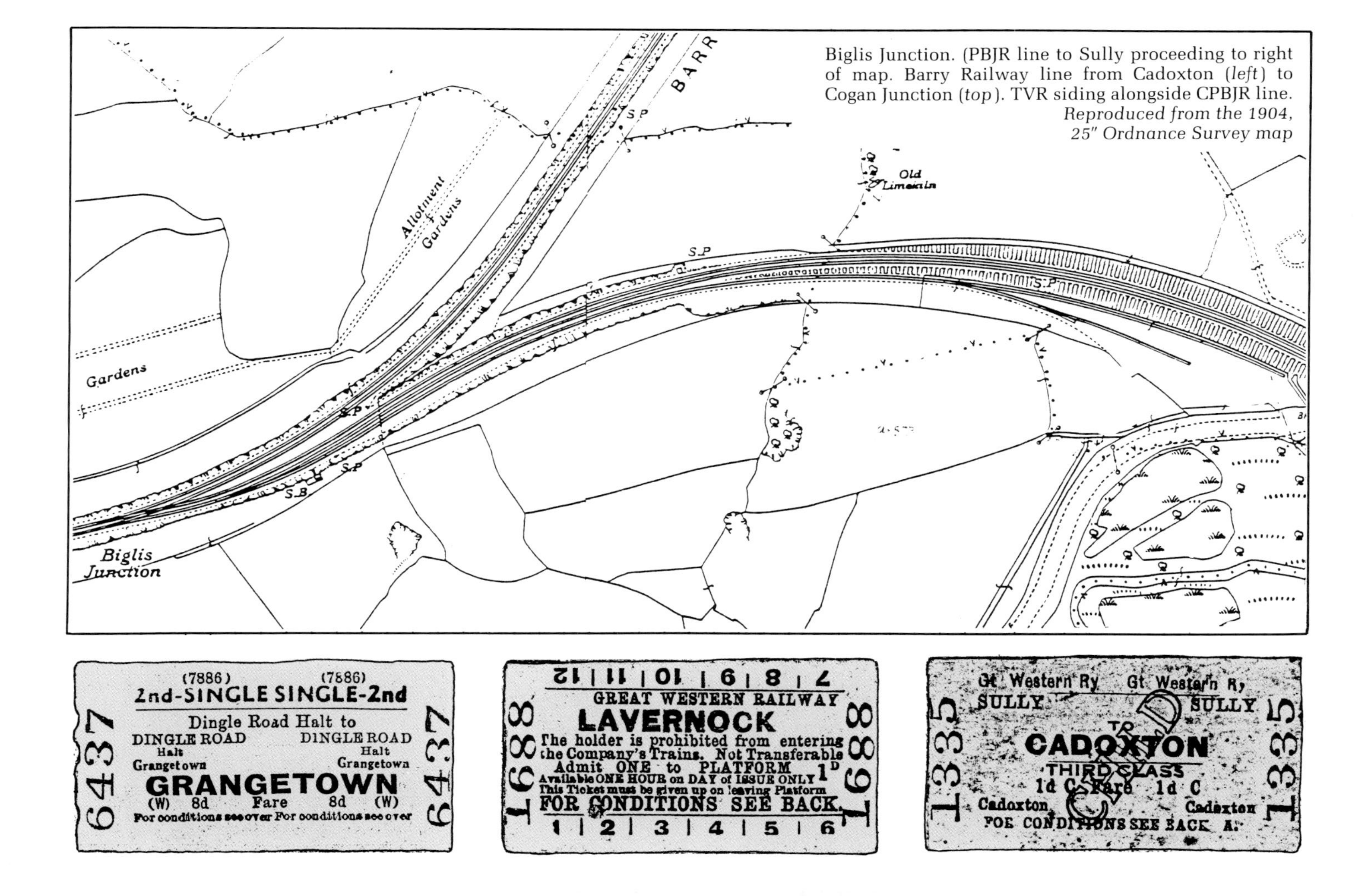

Biglis Junction. (PBJR line to Sully proceeding to right of map. Barry Railway line from Cadoxton (*left*) to Cogan Junction (*top*). TVR siding alongside CPBJR line. *Reproduced from the 1904, 25" Ordnance Survey map*

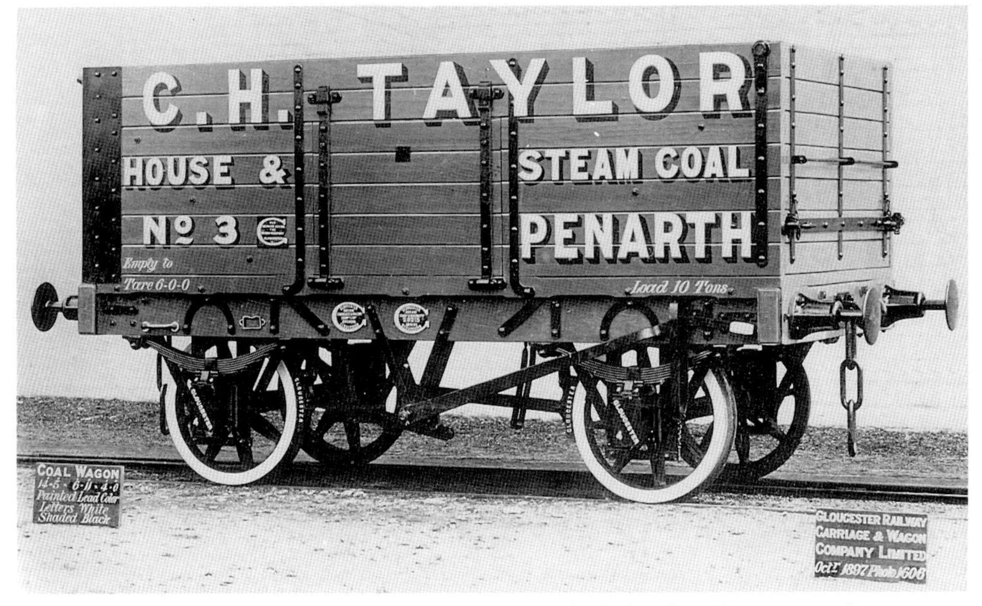

A Penarth-based privately owned coal wagon, built by the Gloucester Railway Carriage and Wagon Co. Ltd in 1897. The wagon was painted in 'lead colour', with white letters shaded black. *Lens of Sutton*

A covered wagon for carrying lime, built for the South Wales Portland Cement and Lime Co. Ltd, Penarth. The wagon was painted in 'lead colour' with white letters shaded red. *Lens of Sutton*

Anyone wishing to get to Cadoxton, or Barry, alighting at Biglis, had to walk across two ploughed fields to get to the road and then almost half a mile along the road to the station. No wonder the few who wished to travel caught a Taff train from Penarth to Penarth Dock, and changed into a Barry train at the adjacent Cogan station.

However such a state of affairs could not be allowed to continue and, following protest meetings held in Penarth, the Taff took the matter to the Railway Commissioners, where on Monday 26th January, 1890 Mr Justice Wills ordered the Barry to make arrangements to receive Taff trains at Cadoxton. He only awarded the Taff £100 nominal damages as in his view they had made no effort to reach agreement with the Barry. However the Barry had to take the principal blame as Parliament had authorised the running powers by the Act of 6th August, 1885, and the Barry's defence that Cadoxton station had not been constructed to accept Taff trains must fail on those grounds.

As a delaying tactic the Barry announced their intention to appeal, and the case was set to be heard before the Master of the Rolls at the Court of Appeal in April 1890. In fact the Barry had commenced erecting separate up and down platforms for the Taff trains at Cadoxton in mid-February, but kept the appeal alive to use it as a lever in its negotiations with the Taff for something far more useful to them – running powers into Cardiff. This was achieved by an agreement dated 19th March, 1890 which gave the Barry running powers for both mineral and passenger traffic over the TVR from Cogan Jn to Penarth Curve South, followed by the Barry Railway Act of 1891 s.30 which extended these powers over the GWR into Cardiff.

Having achieved the running powers agreement with the Taff the Barry withdrew its appeal, stating that the matter had been settled out of court, and the Taff passenger trains finally started running into Cadoxton station on Thursday 22nd May, 1890. As from the same date, the temporary station at Biglis Jn was closed. At no time had the Barry put in a temporary platform on their own line at the junction to make it an interchange point, hence the station was little used and, in later years, its existence was almost forgotten, although the Taff – after demolishing the station – did put in a siding at that point. This led to a small goods shed sited near the Cardiff to Barry road which survived to GWR days, being closed (due to the close proximity of Cadoxton Goods Shed) as from 1st June, 1923.

Before leaving the CPBJR it should be recorded that this was one of the small companies amalgamated with the TVR by the latter's Amalgamations and Capital Act of 26th August, 1889, the actual amalgamation being backdated to take effect from 1st July, 1889. The shareholders received four per cent TVR preference stock to replace their ordinary CPBJR stock holding.

The Barry Railway did not commence using its running powers into Cardiff until the GWR had erected a separate station, alongside the GWR main station, to receive its trains. This was called Riverside Junction station and, on the opening day 14th August, 1893, the 9.18 am Barry train from that junction was derailed on the sharp curve at Cogan Jn. The engine stayed on the track, but several of the carriages were derailed. Little damage was done to TVR track, and all that remains in Taff records is a bill for £19 10s. 4*d*.

TVR auto-train on the down passenger line at Grangetown station, with a vehicle on either side of an auto-fitted 'I' class 4–4–0T. This type of train was introduced in 1907, as described in *Chapter 3*. *Lens of Sutton*

TVR 'O2' class 0–6–2T No. 84 (*left*) on up train at Penarth Town in 1915, with another 0–6–2T approaching on a down train. Of interest are the somersault signals, with two sighting strips on each arm, affixed to Stanwell Road bridge, with, beyond, the excursion platform and approach ramp. *Courtesy Great Western Trust*

which the Barry received from that company for the repair work they had to do.

As far as can be traced, the Taff did not use Riverside Junction station until after the GWR had converted the whole of the Riverside Branch into a passenger line with a terminus station near the docks, called Clarence Road. Barry Railway trains were extended to Clarence Road as from Monday 2nd April, 1894, and the Taff started using both Riverside Junction and Clarence Road stations as from 1st May. The Taff trains between Penarth and their own main line at Queen Street still used the main GWR station of course and, with the increasing traffic at that station, caused considerable concern to the GWR by having to cross over their main line to get to the TVR line. Hence with the down bay out of use now that the Taff local trains used the Riverside Branch, the opportunity was taken to rebuild that side of the GWR station. A fly-over was constructed between Queen Street and the GWR station with separate platforms for Taff trains at the latter station and independent lines which continued to Penarth Curve East Jn enabling Taff trains to pass through the GWR station without going over any section of the GWR main line. These separate lines and the fly-over were first brought into use on 7th June, 1896.

The Barry Railway commenced using their running powers for mineral traffic between Cogan Jn and Penarth Curve South Jn on 1st November, 1896. Lucrative coal traffic was taken from the Taff at Penarth Curve and diverted to Barry Dock. However, the ever-increasing traffic over the section with running powers – the Barry were running 11 passenger trains each way daily over it as well as the coal traffic – led them to promote a Bill in the 1897 Session to secure powers to construct a separate line from Cogan to the GWR at Riverside Jn, maintaining a connection with the Taff near Penarth Curve North for the coal traffic. Whether the Barry really intended to construct the line is a matter of doubt, but it did act as a spur to get the Taff to quadruple their line over the offending section. On the Taff's promise the Barry did not press their Bill, although the quadrupled track was not completed until 1904, as some heavy engineering work was involved. It was necessary to construct a new bridge, for the fourth track, over the river Ely, the old three road bridge alongside being partially reconstructed at the same time. Another large project was the renewal of Grangetown station, where the two platform station was demolished and an island platform for the up and down passenger lines erected, the two mineral lines being on the eastern side and feeding directly into Llandough sidings, or the harbour branch. The bridges at Grangetown station and near Penarth Curve South Jn also had to be rebuilt to suit the new track layout.

Due to the rail link with Cardiff the population of Penarth had, as expected, increased considerably from the 4,000-odd in 1878 to 12,422 in 1891 and to 14,228 in 1901. Initially the housing had mainly been built around the dock, but the rail link caused this to extend over the headland towards the sea shore, making the *new* Penarth a most desirable dormitory town for businessmen working in Cardiff. It also became very popular as a seaside resort, to which people from both far and near flocked in the summer months. A pier, for paddle steamers plying to and fro across the Bristol

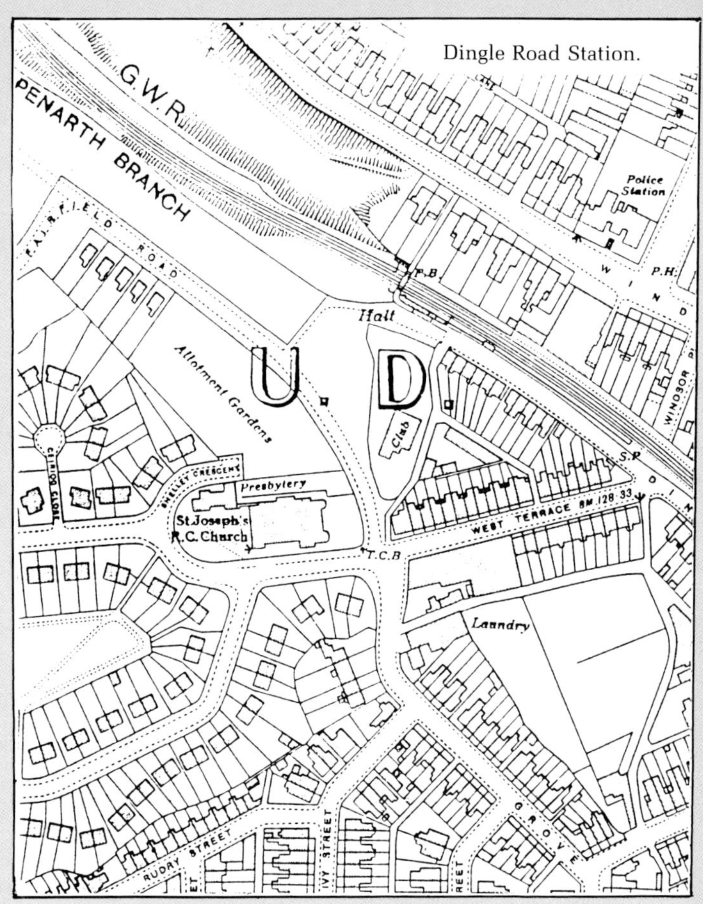

Dingle Road Station.

Both reproduced from the 1904, 25" Ordnance Survey map.

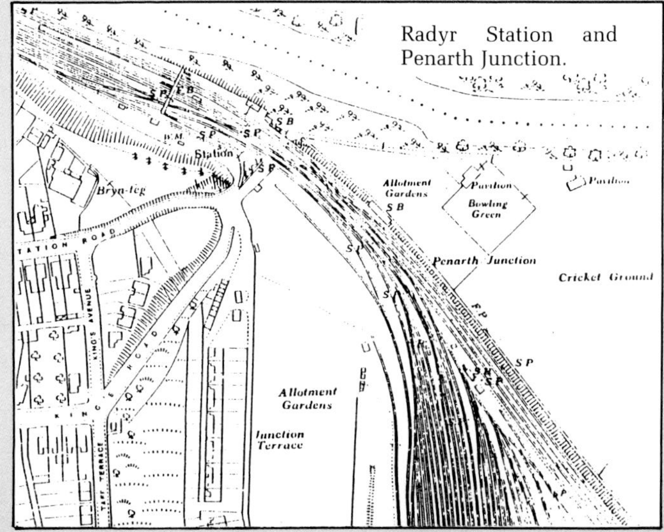

Radyr Station and Penarth Junction.

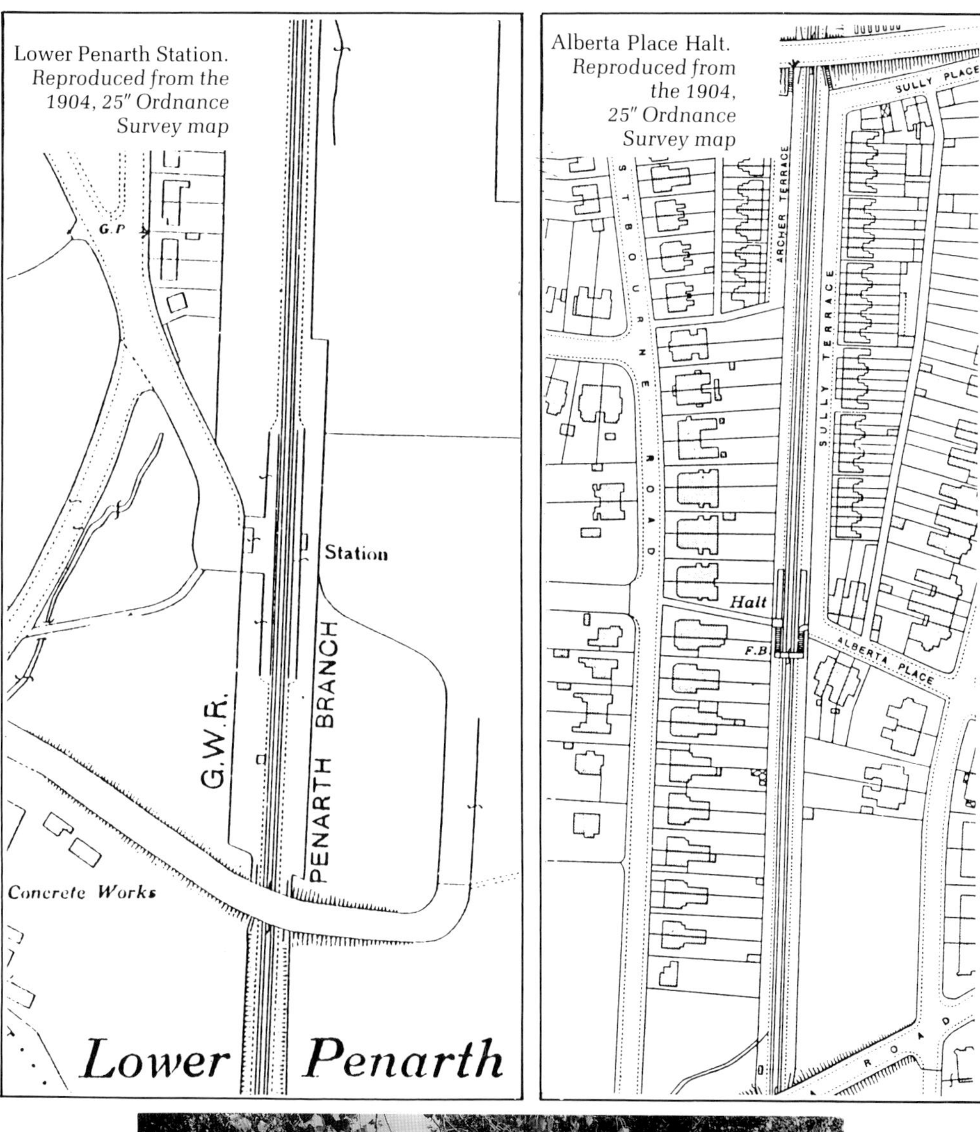

Lower Penarth Station. *Reproduced from the 1904, 25″ Ordnance Survey map*

Alberta Place Halt. *Reproduced from the 1904, 25″ Ordnance Survey map*

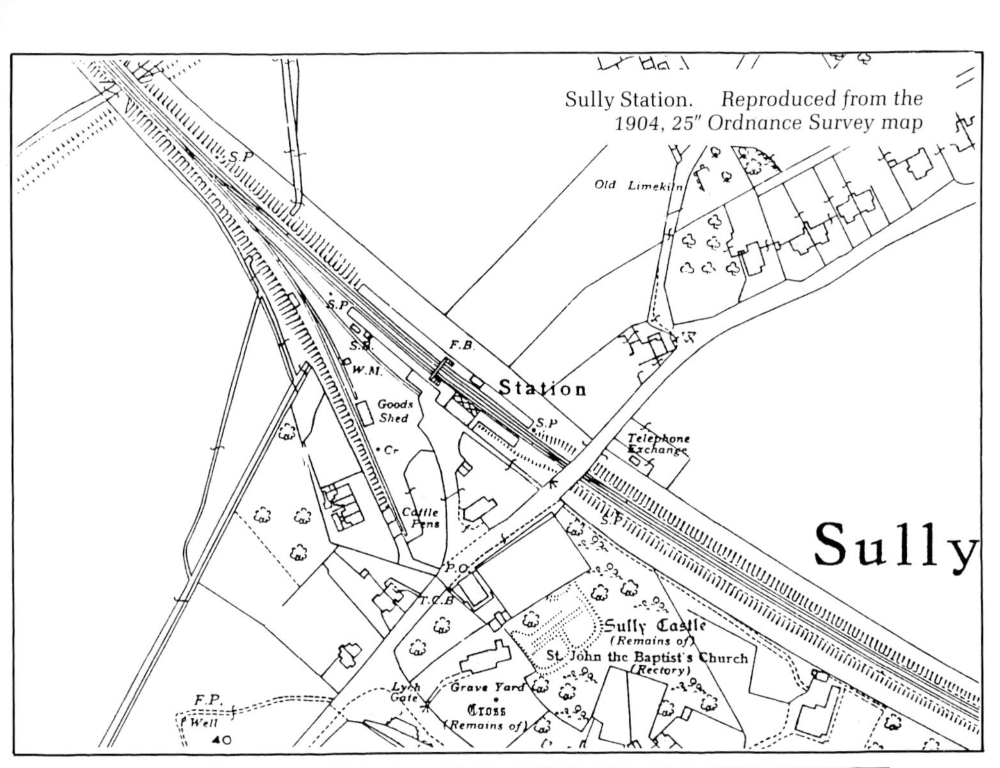

Sully Station. *Reproduced from the 1904, 25" Ordnance Survey map*

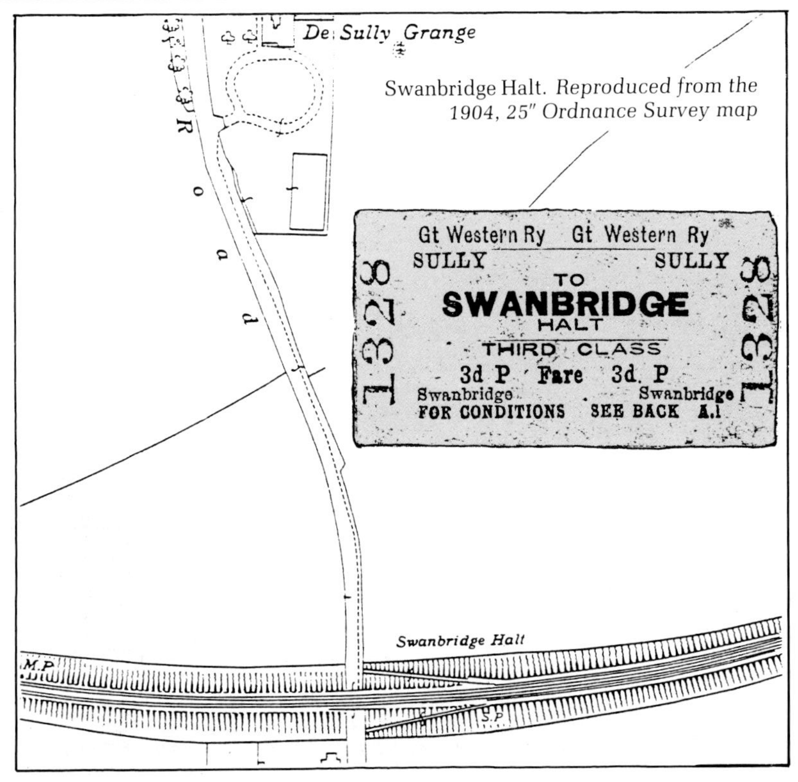

Swanbridge Halt. *Reproduced from the 1904, 25" Ordnance Survey map*

Channel, was added in 1894 to link the seaside resorts on both sides of the channel, and the seafront rapidly acquired the usual amenities of a progressive seaside resort. Despite the fairly close proximity of the dock, the headland screened off the sight of same to those people who spent their leisure hours at the sea shore at Penarth. Hence the passenger traffic expanded by leaps and bounds and, in the early years of the century, the number of tickets issued at Penarth equalled those issued at the Taff's main station at Cardiff Queen Street.

This expansion caused further stations to be erected. The first was at Lower Penarth, one mile south of Penarth Town station on the line to Cadoxton, near which the Glamorgan Golf Club had set out a course. A private opening for members of the golf club took place on 2nd January, 1897, followed by its public opening on Monday 1st February. When rail motors – a passenger carriage combined with a small steam propulsion unit – were introduced on the Taff as from 26th December, 1903, the inaugural service was between Cardiff and Penarth. This proved so popular that a second car was added in 1904 and certain of the services were extended over the coast route to Cadoxton. 'Motor platforms' were added as shown below; the first two or three were originally lineside stops, with nameboards, lighting and little else, the car guard operating folding steps on the cars for the passengers to entrain or alight, and unlocking and locking the gate to the public roadway:

	Between	*Opened*
Llandough Platform	Grangetown and Penarth Dock	13th June, 1904
Dingle Road Platform	Penarth Dock and Penarth	1st March, 1904
Alberta Place Platform	Penarth and Lower Penarth	19th September, 1904
Swanbridge Platform	Lavernock and Sully	June 1906

The platforms proved so popular that, except at Llandough, platforms and shelters were later provided, also the traffic increase led to two special six-wheeled trailer cars being constructed in 1905 for use with the cars and this, to a large extent, proved their downfall. The Taff was no easy line for the diminutive engines powering the cars, and the Penarth section with its gradient of 1 in 40 from near Penarth Dock station for 45 chains up the headland towards Penarth Town station was no exception. Dingle Road platform was sited on this gradient and there were several reports of cars being stuck at the platform on the run to Penarth, being unable to get away with the added weight of a loaded trailer car behind. There were also gradients of 1 in 45, 48, 60 and 69 between Penarth and Lavernock, but on this section the cars were not normally so heavily laden. The trailer cars also meant the steam cars had to 'run-round' at each terminus, whereas the cars on their own could be driven from either end, hence valuable time was wasted on the short runs such as Cardiff to Penarth.

This resulted in auto-trains being introduced in 1907, initially one large trailer car at each end of a small locomotive, capable of being driven from either end. Several of the platforms had to be lengthened to suit and this was again necessary in 1910 when four car auto-trains were introduced, with two cars at each end of the locomotive. Llandough Platform was little altered,

Lower Penarth station, looking towards Penarth. *Lens of Sutton*

TVR steam motor car No. 6 (with six-wheel coach attached).
The National Museum of Wales

A TVR train in the Barry Railway station at Cadoxton, presumably on arrival from Cardiff via Penarth, hauled by 'C' class 4–4–2T No. 171.
Courtesy Great Western Trust

Swanbridge Halt, looking towards Penarth, photographed in its final years.
Lens of Sutton

A four-car auto-train, with motive power provided by an auto-fitted 'C' class 4–4–2T, standing at the down platform at Penarth Town in later TVR days.
G.H.W. Clifford (R.C. Riley Collection)

and no trains were allowed to stop there during the hours of darkness. It closed entirely as from 1st June, 1918. On the one side of this platform were the very busy coal storage sidings already mentioned, and as no footbridge was provided passengers had to cross the up main line to get to the public road, hence passengers were not allowed to alight from down cars if any train was in the section on the up side. As the platform was only 31 chains north of Penarth Dock station its early closure was not surprising.

In the early years of the century, an excursion platform was opened on the up side at Penarth Town, separated from the existing station by the road bridge at the north end. This platform was authorised on 24th October, 1905 and brought into use about April/May 1906, although the actual date was not recorded. It was used until 1939, but closed during the war except for one or two military specials, and demolished about 1946.

One further platform was opened by the Taff on the Penarth lines on 2nd November, 1912. This was Ninian Park, on the PHDR main line just west of Penarth Curve North Jn. This section had previously only been used for mineral and goods traffic and the new station, although classed as a 'Motor Platform', was actually some 300 ft in length and erected to suit ordinary trains as well as cars and auto trains. It was authorised as 'Leckwith Road Pleasure Platform' but as Ninian Park, the home of Cardiff City football club, stood alongside the name was changed just prior to opening. This was done for ease of identification, and not because the Taff management had doubts whether the word 'pleasure' was always a correct definition of the fare served up on Saturday afternoons at Ninian Park! At the time the platform opened Cardiff City was not a well known football club, and the original name doubtless referred to the nearby parks and walks within easy reach of the platform. When opened only one platform was provided – on the down side from the PHDR point of view (i.e. alongside the track carrying traffic from the valleys and Radyr). The platform was normally only used for football traffic, the opening day being when the 'City' were playing Pontypridd in a qualifying round of the FA Cup which, incidentally, they won by two goals to one.

During Taff days some unusual passenger workings resulted from the opening of the platform. Most football excursions from the valleys used the Penarth line from Penarth Jn (Radyr) to the platform, and this route was also used by Taff auto-train excursions from Cardiff Queen St which took the main line to Radyr, where they reversed over the Penarth line to the football platform. These trains called at Woodville Road and Maindy platforms also Llandaff and Radyr stations on the main line.

Although at this time Ninian Park was the only passenger 'station' on the northern section of the PHDR between Radyr and Penarth Curves, and passenger trains ran over this section only on special occasions such as football matches, this four miles of line was punctuated by four points of importance to freight traffic.

Surveying these from the Radyr end, Radyr Quarry Junction has already been mentioned in connection with the 1900 Llandaff Loop, while there was a rail-connected quarry here from earlier times. Next was Waterhall Junction, also referred to previously in the context of the 'Llantrisant No. 1

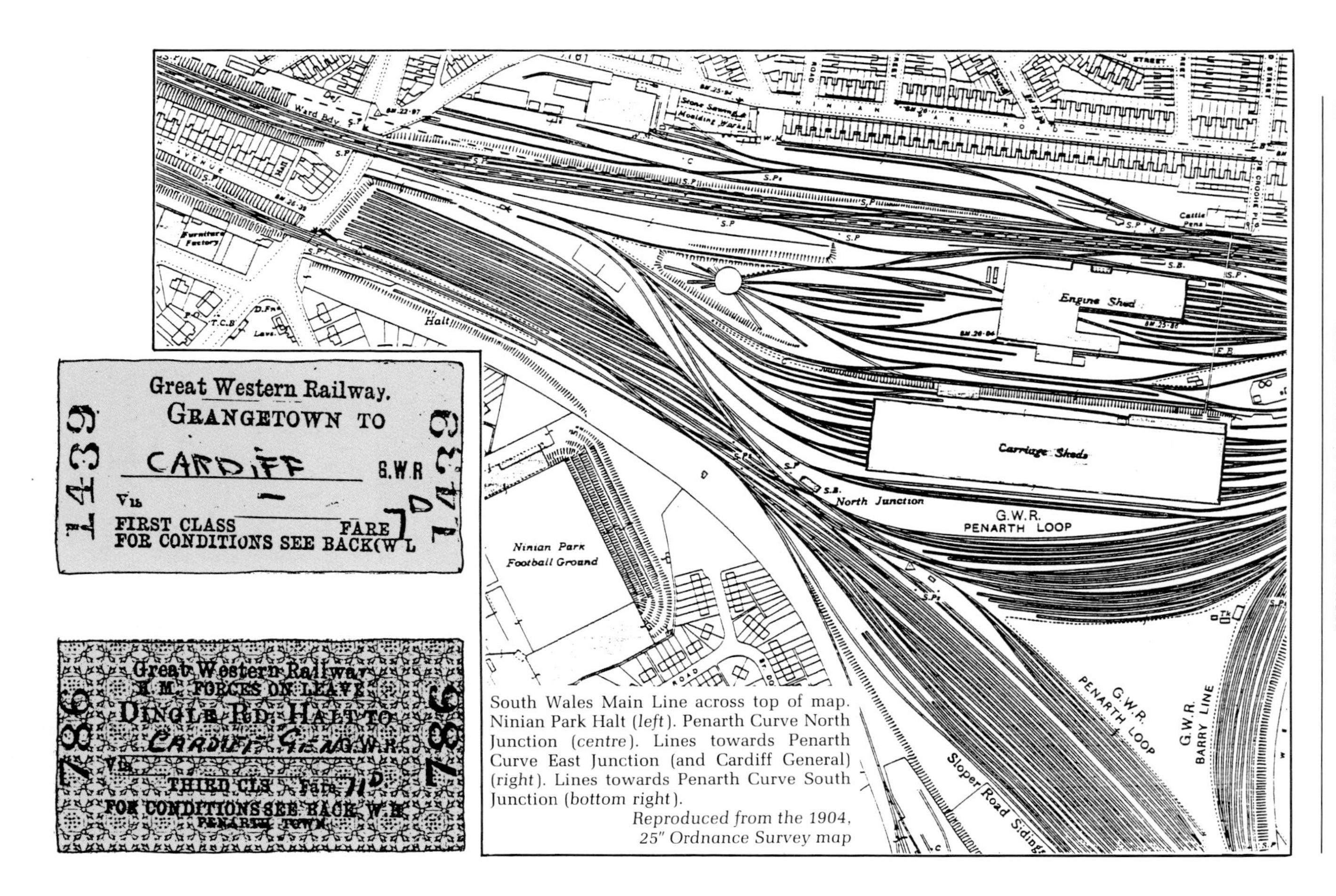

South Wales Main Line across top of map. Ninian Park Halt (*left*). Penarth Curve North Junction (*centre*). Lines towards Penarth Curve East Junction (and Cardiff General) (*right*). Lines towards Penarth Curve South Junction (*bottom right*).

Reproduced from the 1904, 25" Ordnance Survey map

T.V.R.

A DAY at PENARTH

On MONDAY, AUGUST 29,

A DAY EXCURSION

WILL BE RUN TO

PENARTH

FROM	AT	RETURN FARES 3RD CLASS	
	A.M.	S.	D.
Maerdy	8 55	3	9
Ferndale	9 0	3	6
Tylorstown	9 5	3	3
Ynishir	9 10	3	0
Porth	9 20	3	0
Trehafod	9 25	2	9
Pontypridd	9 30	2	6
Treforest	9 35	2	3
Taffs Well	9 45	1	6
Radyr	9 50	1	3

The Return Train will leave PENARTH at 8.30 p.m. the same day.

Children under three years of age, free; three and under twelve, half price. No luggage allowed.

Tickets may be obtained in advance at the Stations.

Excursion Tickets are only available to and from the Stations named upon them. Should an Excursion Ticket be used for any other Station than those named upon it, or by any other train than as specified above, it will be rendered void, and therefore the fare paid will be liable to forfeiture, and the full Ordinary fare will become chargeable. The tickets are not transferable.

CARDIFF, August, 1921.

E. A. PROSSER,
General Manager.

Handbill advertising excursions to Penarth by the TVR in 1921.
The National Museum of Wales, Harris Collection

On Monday, April 7th, and Saturdays, April 12th and 26th,

EXCURSIONS TO

NINIAN PARK

(Provided the Matches are played)

FROM	Monday, April 7th AT	Saturdays, April 12th & 26th, AT	Return Fares, Third Class
	P.M.	P.M.	s. d.
Merthyr	4 25	1 30	2 11
Pentrebach	4 [illegible]	[illegible]	2 9
Troedyrhiw	4 3[illegible]	1 40	2 7
Merthyr Vale	4 40	1 45	2 5
Quakers Y'rd (L.L.) ...	4 45	1 55	2 1
Aberdare (T.V.) ...	4 5	1 25	2 10
Aberaman	4 10	1 30	2 8
M'ntain Ash (T.V.) ...	4 20	1 35	2 5
Penrhiwceiber (T.V.) ...	4 25	1 40	2 2
Ynysybwl	4 [illegible]	1 [illegible]	2 0
[illegible] (T.V.) ...	4 0	2 55	1 10
[illegible] ...	4 10	1 10	1 9
[illegible] ...	4 [illegible]	2 0	1 11
[illegible]pridd (T.V.) ...	[illegible]	2 10	1 6
[illegible]	3 55	‡12 55	1 11
Llantwit	4 5	1 5	1 7

FROM	Monday, April 7th AT	Saturdays, April 12th & 26th AT	Return Fares, Third Class
	P.M.	P.M.	s. d.
Church Village ...	4 1[illegible]	[illegible] 9	1 5
Treherbert	4 5	1 15	2 10
Treorchy	4 10	1 20	2 8
Ystrad	4 15	1 25	2 6
Llwynypia	4 20	1 30	2 3
Tonypandy	4 25	1 35	2 1
Dinas	4 30	1 40	2 1
Maerdy	3 50	1 [illegible]	2 8
Ferndale	3 55	1 10	2 5
Tylorstown	4 0	1 20	2 2
Ynyshir	4 5	1 25	2 0
Porth	[illegible]	1 45	1 11
Trehafod	[illegible]	1 50	1 9
Treforest	[illegible]	2 0	1 5
Taffs Well	[illegible]	2 10	0 9
Radyr	[illegible]	[illegible]	[illegible] 9

Passengers return from Cardiff (Queen Street) Station as under—
Radyr, Taffs Well, Treforest, Pontypridd and Rhondda and Ferndale Branches—Any Ordinary train also at 7.5, [illegible], 8.50, 9.5, 9.40 & 11.10 p.m.
Aberdare and Merthyr Branches " " 7.40, 8.50, 9.30, & 11.0 p.m.
Llantwit, Church Village, and Cross Inn—Any ordinary train—Last train 9.20 p.m.
Ynysybwl ... ... " " Last train 9.45 p.m.
Nelson (T.V.) and Cilfynydd—Any ordinary train, also at 7.50, 9.20 and 9.45 p.m.
Except Dinas. ‡ Not on April 7th.

Sunday Evening Concerts at the Capitol, Queen St. at 8.15 p.m.

DOORS OPEN AT 7.30 P.M.

For Attractions at the Capitol and further particulars, see separate announcement.

ON EACH SUNDAY DURING APRIL,

1st. & 3rd. Class Cheap Tickets will be issued to CARDIFF

FROM	AT			Return Fares First Class	Return Fares Third Class	Passengers return
	a.m.	p.m.	p.m.	s. d.	s. d.	
Pontypridd (T.V.)	8 55	12 11	5 3	2 6	1 6	From Cardiff (Queen St.) by any train also by special at 10.20 p.m.
Treforest (T.V.)	8 59	12 15	5 7	2 5	1 5	
Taffs Well..	9 9	12 25	5 17	1 3	0 9	
Radyr ...	9 14	12 30	5 22	0 10	0 6	
Llandaff ...	9 18	12 34	5 26	0 10	0 6	
Caerphilly ..	Any train			1 8	1 0	From Cardiff (Rhy) by any train also by special at
Llanishen				0 1[illegible]	0 6	

FROM	AT	Return Fares First Class	Return Fares Third Class	Passengers return
		s. d.	s. d.	
Barry Island	Any train up to 7.30 p.m.	2 1	1 3	From Cardiff (Gen) by any train.
Barry ...		1 10	1 1	
Barry Docks		1 6	0 11	
Cadoxton ...		1 5	0 10	
Dinas Powis		1 3	0 9	
Cogan ...		0 10	0 6	
Penarth ...		0 10	0 6	From Cardiff (Gen.) by any train.
Penarth Dock		0 10	0 6	

An early GWR handbill advertising excursions to Ninian Park in April 1924.
The National Museum of Wales, Harris Collection

The TVR Ely Goods Yard signal box, photographed in the early 1950s, showing in the foreground the connection to Ely (Fairwater Road) goods yard. The somersault signals are Ely Goods Yard up home with Waterhall Junction up distant below. The down signal, visible in the background, is of GWR pattern. The signal box was removed on 10th February, 1957, and was located between the present-day Waun-gron Park and Fairwater stations.
N.S. Carey

TVR up line somersault signal at Ely Paper Mills, together with a TVR revolving shunt signal on the 'doll' below, photographed in the 1950s.
N.S. Carey

Railway': there was a goods yard here, too, reached from the Llantrisant line. Less than a ½-mile further south, between the present-day Fairwater and Waun-gron Park stations, were Ely Goods Yard and signal box, on the up side of the line. Then, after the Penarth line had crossed over the GWR South Wales Main Line there came, also on the up side, Ely Paper Mills sidings, with Ely Paper Mills signal box on the opposite side of the line.

Reverting to Ninian Park Platform, further changes were to come, but these occurred during the Great Western Railway and British Rail eras, and are therefore described in the next chapter which takes the story of the Taff Vale lines to Penarth into the years of change from 1922 onwards.

TVR Penarth Town Signal box, photographed on 22nd May, 1964. *I.L. Wright*

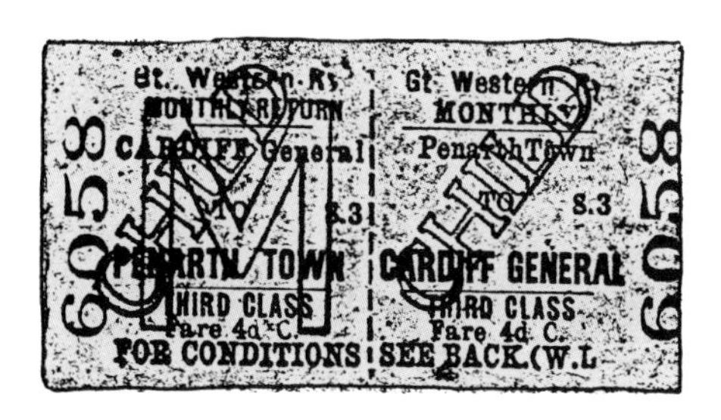

Ex-TVR 'A' class 0–6–2T No. 356 (TVR No. 123) at Penarth Town on a down train in early GWR days. *H.T. Hobbs (R.C. Riley Collection)*

A down train entering Dingle Road in early GWR days, hauled by ex-TVR 'A' class 0–6–2T No. 345 (TVR No. 20). *H.T. Hobbs (R.C. Riley Collection)*

An up passenger train approaching Radyr in early GWR days, hauled by an ex-TVR 'A' class 0–6–2T. The train, arriving from the Cardiff Queen Street and Llandaff main line, is passing over the junction with the PHDR line, which diverges right, as seen by the cameraman. *Courtesy of Great Western Trust*

An up auto train at Alberta Place in 1923, propelled by ex-TVR 'C' class 4–4–2T No. 1303 (TVR No. 172), and formed of two ex-TVR auto trailers.

H.T. Hobbs (R.C. Riley Collection)

Chapter Two

The years of change since 1922

As mentioned in the previous chapter, the Penarth Harbour, Dock and Railway (PHDR), the Penarth Extension Railway (PER), and the Taff Vale Railway (TVR), were amongst those amalgamated with the Great Western Railway as from 1922/23 as part of the 'grouping' of Britain's many railways into four large companies, which were to continue in being until nationalisation in 1948.

By this grouping process, the Great Western, which had already owned the main trunk route through South Wales since 1863, now controlled as from 1922/23 not only almost all the railways in South Wales, but also the harbours and docks owned by the former independent companies such as the Taff Vale and the Barry: including, of course, the harbour and dock at Penarth.

At the same time, significant changes in trading conditions, and in the growth and evolution of transport, were in the immediate offing.

As an indication of things remaining unchanged for a while, however, passenger traffic returns issued by the GWR for the year 1923 revealed that Penarth Town station, together with Dingle Road and Alberta Place Halts, were still issuing more tickets than Cardiff Queen St station, but the receipts were somewhat less as the vast majority of Penarth's tickets were for the short distance to Cardiff only. At that time Penarth was issuing more passenger tickets than any ex-TVR station except Pontypridd. The relevant 1923 returns were:

	Passenger tickets issued	*Season tickets*	*Passenger receipts*
Penarth Town*	532,713	7,357	£36,785
Cardiff Queen St	507,216	3,379	£43,252

*including Dingle Road and Alberta Place Halts.

During the same year Penarth Dock station issued 91,077 tickets plus 588 season tickets, with receipts of £2,831.

Picking up yet again the story of Ninian Park Platform, in 1920 Cardiff City were elected to Division 2 of the Football League, and Ninian Park Platform assumed a greater degree of importance. Following the club's rise to fame by winning the FA Cup in 1927, it was decided to enlarge the platform but this was held in abeyance until the major reconstruction of Cardiff GWR station and approach lines between 1931 and 1934. Ninian Park Platform was then extended to 500 ft in length, and a second similar platform added for the up line. In 1932 a short link between the GWR main line and the Penarth line was put in at Leckwith Jn immediately west of Ninian Park Platform. Besides being useful for mineral traffic from the GWR main line west of Cardiff to Penarth Dock, it also enabled occasional main line football excursions from the west to go to the platform direct. At the same time football excursions from the GWR main line eastwards reached the platform via Penarth Curve North, while excursions from the Barry line via Penarth Curve South and North junctions were not unknown.

A general view of Penarth Docks. *Courtesy Great Western Railway Magazine*

In 1934 a series of summer Sunday auto-train excursions was introduced to Barry Island from St Fagans station, on the GWR main line, via Ninian Park. These used the new crossover at Leckwith Jn and were routed both via Penarth and the former Barry Railway route via Dinas Powys. These were the first non-football excursions known to have called at Ninian Park. In the later 1930s some Sunday excursions from Newport to Porthcawl were also routed via Ninian Park and Leckwith Jn, but all these excursions were withdrawn with the outbreak of war on 3rd September, 1939.

Returning to the dock traffic after the GWR had taken control of the South Wales ports in 1922, the trade at Penarth increased in the post-war boom to 3,440,233 tons of coal exported in 1923, but afterwards recession set in. In 1925 the figures were only 2,453,848 tons and the following year was a complete disaster for the coal export trade. The General Strike started at the beginning of May 1926 and, although this collapsed after about ten days, the miners remained on strike until the end of November. The tonnage of coal shipped at Penarth that year was only 1,054,557. In 1927 the figure rose to just over two million tons, but that was followed by the long depression which sounded the death knell to Penarth as a port.

By February 1929 the trade had so diminished that Penarth Dock engine shed was closed, the passenger engines were transferred to Cardiff Cathays, whilst the mineral engines were shared between Barry and Cardiff Docks sheds. Coal exports continued to diminish and Penarth Dock was temporarily closed to commercial shipping as from 6th July, 1936. It remained open for shipping requiring laying up berths in the dock, also for access to ships for repair at Penarth Pontoon. The Ely harbour remained open for coal shipment and oil imports; the trade gradually improved from a total import/export of 397,227 tons in 1937 to 542,974 tons in 1939. Of that total no less than 494,332 tons was coal export.

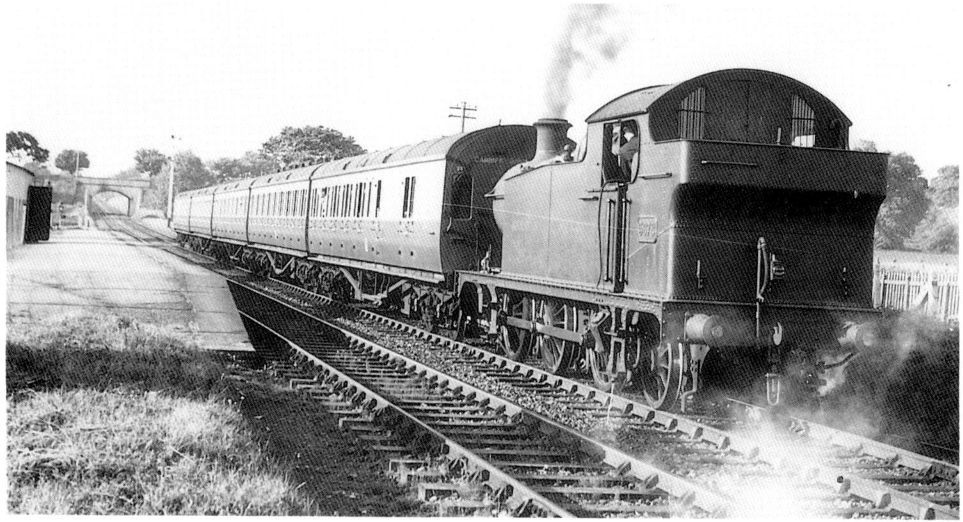

GWR 0–6–2T No. 5676 on a down train of GWR non-corridor stock at Lower Penarth in 1937. *B.J. Miller Collection*

A down train, with two clerestory roofed coaches at the rear, leaving Lower Penarth in 1937 hauled by GWR 0–6–2T No. 6692. *B.J. Miller Collection*

A down train entering Lavernock station in August 1925, formed of ex-TVR 'M' class 0–6–2T No. 507 (TVR No. 50) hauling two ex-TVR auto-trailers. *B.J. Miller Collection*

Sunday excursion train in Swanbridge cutting on the Penarth–Cadoxton CPBJR line during GWR days, with a GWR 56XX/66XX class 0–6–2T hauling an interesting collection of rolling stock. *H.T. Hobbs (R.C. Riley Collection)*

A view north-west from Penarth Curve South Junction signal box taken on 27th September, 1933 at the time of the layout alterations carried out by the GWR in the Cardiff General and Canton areas. From the junction (*bottom right*) the line to the left is the PHDR route towards Radyr, with Penarth Curve North Junction signal box in the middle distance: while the line to the right is that to Penarth Curve East Junction and Cardiff General station. Beyond (*right*) on the farther side of the Penarth Curves triangular layout, is Canton depot. Note loaded coal wagons in the sidings, left. *National Museum of Wales*

A GWR publicity photograph of Penarth promenade and pier, taken in June 1929.
The National Museum of Wales

A GWR publicity photograph of St. Mary's Well Bay (which was reached from Lavernock station) also taken in June 1929. *The National Museum of Wales*

Corresponding with the dock trade, passenger traffic – apart from season tickets – also slumped between 1923 and World War II. By 1933 the number of ordinary tickets issued at Penarth had fallen to 372,531, a drop of 30 per cent. Even so, the policy of using Penarth as a dormitory town for Cardiff increased in popularity and season tickets had risen to 9,439. The population at Penarth in 1931 was 17,710. Nevertheless the challenge of road transport, both public and private, gradually took its toll, and by 1938 ordinary tickets had dropped to 275,024 – almost half the 1923 total. Rather surprisingly, season tickets were even more popular, and had increased, slightly, to 10,041. Throughout the period from 1923 to 1939 there was a service of at least 40 trains running between Penarth and Cardiff in each direction on weekdays, and this was only reduced to 32 each way in the emergency war timetable which operated as from 25th September, 1939, the cut being much less severe than on many other branch lines.

Throughout the GWR period, and indeed continuing into early British Railways days from 1948 onwards, the general pattern of the Taff Vale timetable, in relation to the Penarth services remained unaltered, with three basic services operating in the Penarth area. These were:

1) Most of the main line passenger services from the Taff valley terminated at Penarth.
2) A local passenger service between Penarth and Cardiff, terminating at either Riverside or Clarence Road stations at Cardiff.
3) A local service between Penarth and Cadoxton, with a few of these trains extending as an addition to the local service to Cardiff.

It should be mentioned that in 1932/3 the old Riverside Junction station at Cardiff was demolished and replaced by a new island platform. The latter still retained the name Cardiff Riverside until 23rd October, 1940 when it was combined with Cardiff General Station to form platforms 8 and 9 of that station.

The needs of World War II caused a temporary re-opening of Penarth dock in July 1940. This was for general war traffic, coal and oil still being handled at the harbour. The peak war year was 1943 when the total trade at both dock and harbour was 546,940 tons, of which coal export at the harbour contributed 490,227 tons. Thus it was no surprise when the dock again closed to commercial shipping in 1947. As before, access was allowed to Penarth Pontoon and ships, which included surplus Navy vessels, were laid up at the dock. Finally the dock closed to shipping in 1963 and has since been partly filled in. The Ely harbour dealt with an ever-diminishing coal trade until 31st December, 1962, but did not close completely until August 1985 with the cessation of oil and petroleum products traffic.

By the Transport Act of 1947, Britain's railways were nationalised as from 1st January, 1948. They came under the control of the British Transport Commission, with the railways managed by the Railway Executive and known as British Railways (BR), while the docks and harbours were looked after by the Docks and Inland Waterways Executive. It is convenient here to summarise subsequent changes. The British Transport Commission was later dissolved, and from 1963 there has existed the British Railways Board

The first cargo of Esparto Grass to arrive for many years, being discharged at Penarth Dock. *Courtesy GWR Magazine*

An aerial view of the mouth of the river Ely in the 1950s, with the Tidal Harbour on the left bank, and Penarth Dock to the right. Upper right, is part of the town of Penarth, and towards the bottom of the picture, right, is Cogan Junction with its former TVR and GWR signal boxes. *The National Museum of Wales*

Ex-GWR 56XX 0–6–2T with an up freight train between Waterhall Junction (visible in background) and the site of the present day Danescourt station, in the early 1960s.
A.F. Smith, Peter Rowe (Printers), Cardiff

Ex-GWR 0–6–2T No. 5614 restarting from Penarth Curve sidings with a train of empty mineral wagons from Barry Docks to the Rhondda Valley via the PHDR route to Radyr on 24th September, 1960. The train also includes two empty engineering department vehicles immediately behind the locomotive. On the left is Penarth Curve North Junction signal box.
J. Hodge

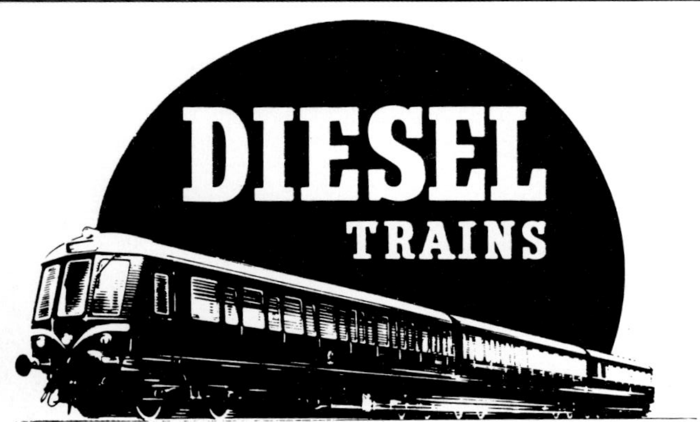

Photograph of a dieselisation poster issued by British Railways, Western Region, in

	Fare—2nd class return
PENARTH	3/3
LAVERNOCK	4/-
SWANBRIDGE	4/3
SULLY	4/3

Out by any train at or after 9.30 back by any train same day changing at Cardiff General each way.

Convenient departures—

Out—Mondays to Saturdays

		SX	SO	SX	SO	SO	SX	SO
Newport	d	10 31	10 23	11 36	11 27	12 05	12 26	12 30
Penarth	a	11 08		12 11		12 45	13 14	
Lavernock	a	11 14		12 24		12 53	13 24	
Swanbridge Halt	a	11 18		12 28		12 56	13 27	
Sully	a	11 21		12 31		12 59	13 31	

		SX	SO	SX	SO
Newport	d	13 17	13 05	14 14	14 19
Penarth	a	14 17		14 58	
Lavernock	a	14 25		15 07	
Swanbridge Halt	a	14 29		15 11	
Sully	a	14 32		15 14	

Come back—Mondays to Saturdays

Sully	d	16 21	16 40	17 10	18 21	18 55	19 24	19 49
Swanbridge Halt	d	16 25	16 44	17 14	18 25	18 59	19 28	19 53
Lavernock	d	16 28	16 47	17 18	18 29	19 02	19 32	19 58
Penarth	d	16 35	16 59	17 25	18 35	19 08	19 40	20 10
Newport	a	SX 17 28	SX 17 43	18 02	SX 19 13	SX 20 15	SX 20 15	20 55
		SO 17 36	SO 17 45	—	SO 19 15	SO 19 57	SO 20 36	—

Out—Sunday

Newport	d	9 47	10 30	11 19	11 36	12 37	12 52	14 18
Penarth	a	10 52	11 27	12 01	12 30	13 21	14 06	14 51
Lavernock	a	10 58	11 36	12 07	12 36	13 27	14 12	14 57
Swanbridge Halt	a	11 02	11 40	12 11	12 40	13 31	14 16	15 01
Sully	a	11 05	11 43	12 14	12 43	13 24	14 19	15 04

Come back—Sunday

Sully	d	16 11	17 30	18 15	18 55	19 30	—
Swanbridge Halt	d	16 15	17 34	18 19	18 58	19 34	—
Lavernock	d	16 18	17 37	18 22	19 02	19 37	20 43
Penarth	d	16 24	17 43	18 28	19 08	19 43	20 49
Newport	a	17 16	18 17	19 03	19 46	20 15	22 05

Key to timetable
SO—Saturdays only. **SX**—Saturdays excepted.

Train services and cheap fares advertised by British Railways, Western Region, from Newport to Penarth, Lavernock, Swanbridge and Sully during the period 15th June to and the British Transport Docks Board, the last named being 'privatised' as from 1983 as Associated British Ports.

As an indication of passenger traffic levels after World War II, figures recorded for March 1952 show that the daily average of passenger journeys originating at stations on the Penarth lines were 12 at Sully, 17 at Lavernock, 809 at Penarth Town (a figure which included journeys originating at Swanbridge, Lower Penarth and Alberta Place), 638 at Dingle Road, 174 at Penarth Dock and 346 at Grangetown. Originating first class journeys were recorded only at Penarth Town and Dingle Road, with daily averages of 17 journeys and 1 journey respectively: all other journeys were in third class (a nomenclature which did not change to 'second class' until 3rd June, 1956). Season ticket issues recorded for the month were 3 at Sully, 262 at Penarth Town (including any issued at Swanbridge, Lower Penarth and Alberta Place), 229 at Dingle Road, 82 at Penarth Dock and 33 at Grangetown.

In an effort to recapture some of the passenger traffic lost to road competition BR remodelled the former Taff and Barry section timetables as from 21st September, 1953, introducing a regular interval service between the Taff line and Barry Island. To compensate for the loss of most of the Taff valley trains which formerly terminated at Penarth, the local service between Penarth and Cardiff was stepped up to give a service of some 30 trains in each direction on weekdays. The Cadoxton service was maintained much as before with a few trains extending to either Barry or Bridgend.

This remained the pattern for the following decade – which saw the introduction of diesel multiple unit trains in stages as from January 1958, to replace steam traction – but as from 16th March, 1964 Clarence Road station and the Riverside branch were closed entirely, the old Riverside platforms at Cardiff General station being closed to normal passenger traffic (although retained until 1992 for parcel traffic and – for a few years from 1964 – for some Rugby football specials from West Wales). From the same date an hourly interval service was introduced between Penarth and Cardiff, supplemented by extra trains at peak periods, some of these originating from both the Taff and Rhymney valleys. However, on 2nd January, 1967, the regular interval pattern was extended to the Rhymney valley service and from that date these trains were extended to terminate at Penarth.

The first station on the Penarth lines to close under BR ownership was Lower Penarth, as from 14th June, 1954. It had lost its status as a station in February 1934, when the GWR classed it as a halt. The next to go was Penarth Dock, as from 1st January, 1962. The need for this station had rapidly decreased following the first temporary dock closure in 1936, but the GWR retained it despite the close proximity of Cogan station on the Barry line. The economy measures of the early 1960s ended, however, the luxury of two stations standing side by side serving a comparatively small community. Today (1992) the substantial up side buildings at Penarth Dock station alongside Cogan Hill are well preserved, in commercial use by a private firm, Crown House Armoury, who purchased them in 1980.

The general decline in freight traffic by rail in the 1960s rendered considerable track capacity redundant. As a result, on the north side of Penarth, Llandough Sidings were taken out of use as from 6th April, 1965. For several

The exterior of the principal up side buildings at Penarth Dock station, which closed at the beginning of 1962, photographed almost 30 years later, on 19th August, 1991. One year after the photograph was taken, controversy was aroused by the proposal of the present owners of the station buildings to demolish them and substitute a modern three-storey block. *N.W. Sprinks*

Penarth Dock station, looking up the incline towards Dingle Road and Penarth, in 1950. *Courtesy Great Western Trust*

The 12.52 pm Cardiff (Clarence Road) to Cadoxton train, hauled by BR-built (GWR design) 2–6–2T No. 4160, passing the TVR Penarth Cement Works signal box on 20th October, 1958. A TVR somersault signal stands alongside the up line. The CC 'target' indicates a Cathays-based working. *R.O. Tuck*

Ex-Rhymney Railway 'A' class 0–6–2T No. 56, rebuilt with GWR-type boiler, standing at the up platform at Penarth Town in early BR days. *H.T. Hobbs (R.C. Riley Collection)*

A new diesel multiple unit train at Penarth Town station on 30th May, 1958, in the early months of diesel operation. *The National Museum of Wales*

A six-car dmu train, in early green livery with yellow 'whisker' on the cab front, restarting from Dingle Road *en route* for Penarth Town on 7th August, 1961. Of interest are the semaphore distant signal, the 'STOP DEAD' sign for up freight trains descending the incline, and the '2' headcode on the train.
A.F. Smith, Peter Rowe (Printers), Cardiff

years prior to closure these had only been used for storage of empty or crippled wagons.

As from 21st March, 1966 the up and down relief lines were taken out of use between Penarth Curve South and Grangetown, together with the down relief line from Penarth Curve East to Penarth Curve South. This was done in conjunction with the introduction of multiple aspect colour light signalling controlled from the then new Cardiff 'Panel' signal box alongside Cardiff General station, a signal box which remains in service today. As part of the same programme of change, the line from Penarth Curve East to Penarth Curve North was reduced to single track.

Then, in connection with the extension of colour light signalling, controlled from Cardiff Panel box, to include Grangetown, Cogan Junction and Penarth, further changes occurred on the weekend of 11th to 13th February, 1967. The up and down relief lines between Grangetown and Cogan Junction were abolished, although up and down loops were retained at Llandough, immediately north of Cogan Junction. All the lines around Penarth dock were taken out of use, the junction at Cogan simplified, and the line from Cogan Junction to Penarth reduced to single track, with single line control under the Track Circuit Block system. The former up platforms remained in use at Dingle Road and Penarth stations.

As part of the same scheme, stop blocks were placed in the track alongside the up platform at Penarth, dividing it into separate sections, one used by passenger trains from and to the Cardiff direction, and one used by passenger trains from and to Cadoxton, which henceforth operated as a self-contained service without any through workings from or to Cardiff. The former down platform line was taken out of use, but the centre 'through' line was retained as a 'siding' (to use the official terminology) enabling freight trains from Cardiff to work through onto the Cadoxton line to reach the South Wales Portland Cement works located beyond the former Lower Penarth station. Double track was retained between Penarth and Cadoxton, and Penarth Town signal box and some semaphore signals were retained to control the through freights and the Cadoxton passenger trains. The Cardiff passenger trains, as stated in the previous paragraph, were under the control of Cardiff Panel box, while a ground frame controlled the junction between the Cardiff line and the erstwhile centre track, now the new 'siding'.

This, however, was very much a stop-gap measure. Passenger traffic on the Penarth to Cadoxton line dwindled to negligible proportions during the winter months in the 1960s, but the reasonably heavy weekend summer traffic to the seashore at Lavernock and Swanbridge, plus a couple of camp coaches stabled at Lavernock and Sully, kept the line open until after the 1967 season.

Following the usual notices of intention to close, the Penarth–Cadoxton passenger service was withdrawn with effect from 6th May, 1968. This resulted in the closure of Alberta Place, Lavernock, Swanbridge and Sully stations, and the complete closure of the line between Penarth Cement Works and Biglis Junction, Cadoxton, freight services having been withdrawn from Lavernock and Sully stations on 7th October, 1963.

TVR Ely Paper Mills signal box, photographed on 3rd June, 1962, looking towards Ninian Park. Until signalling and layout alterations in the late 1950s/early 1960s it was possible for westbound empty football excursion trains from Ninian Park to 'run round' at this point; thenceforward all such empty trains were disposed of by running on to Radyr. *N.S. Carey*

Cogan Junction, looking towards Penarth, on 8th February, 1967 with preparatory work in hand for the remodelling and resignalling of the junction layout, including the elimination of lines to Penarth Dock and the singling of the line to Penarth (Town). To the left is the ex-TVR box, centre is the ex-GWR box, while the Penarth line continues straight ahead to the right of the picture and the Barry line curves away right by the high retaining wall. *National Museum of Wales*

Cogan Junction, looking towards Penarth (*left*) and Barry (*right*), photographed on 15th November, 1990. The two-car Sprinter dmu is working the 10.45 Penarth–Rhymney service. Cogan station (ex-Barry Railway) is immediately beyond the bridge on the right, while the one-time Penarth Dock station (ex-TVR) was immediately beyond the new bridge spanning the Penarth line, emphasising the close proximity of these two stations when both were open in the years from 1888 to 1961. *N.W. Sprinks*

A single power car for Cadoxton waiting to leave Penarth on the last day of the Penarth–Cadoxton service, 4th May, 1968. Behind the buffer stops separating the platform into two sections (*as described in Chapter 2*) is a three-car dmu set on a Cardiff working. Note that the down platform line has been taken up, the centre track remaining. *D.J. Morgan*

BRITISH RLYS (W) BRITISH RLYS (W)
Penarth Town Penarth Town
929 TO 929
TAFFS WELL
via Cardiff
THIRD CLASS
1/8 H Fare 1/8 H
Taffs Well Taffs Well
FOR CONDITIONS SEE BACK FOR CONDITIONS SEE BACK

A view of the TVR signal box at Penarth Town, together with platform furniture and the front of a dmu bound for Cadoxton, in April 1968. This picture shows that track has not only been lifted from the down platform, but also from the goods yard and carriage sidings. The signal box at this time was controlling only movements on the Cadoxton line. *R.E. Masterman*

A view of Alberta Place, looking towards Lower Penarth. Beyond the concrete footbridge are two road bridges, the farther one carrying Forrest Road, the point at which the reinstatement of the railway, proposed in 1987, would have terminated at a new station. Housing developments block the line beyond. *Lens of Sutton*

An up diesel multiple unit train approaching Swanbridge Halt. *Lens of Sutton*

An up dmu train leaves Sully station in April 1958, passing a TVR somersault signal. *I.L. Wright*

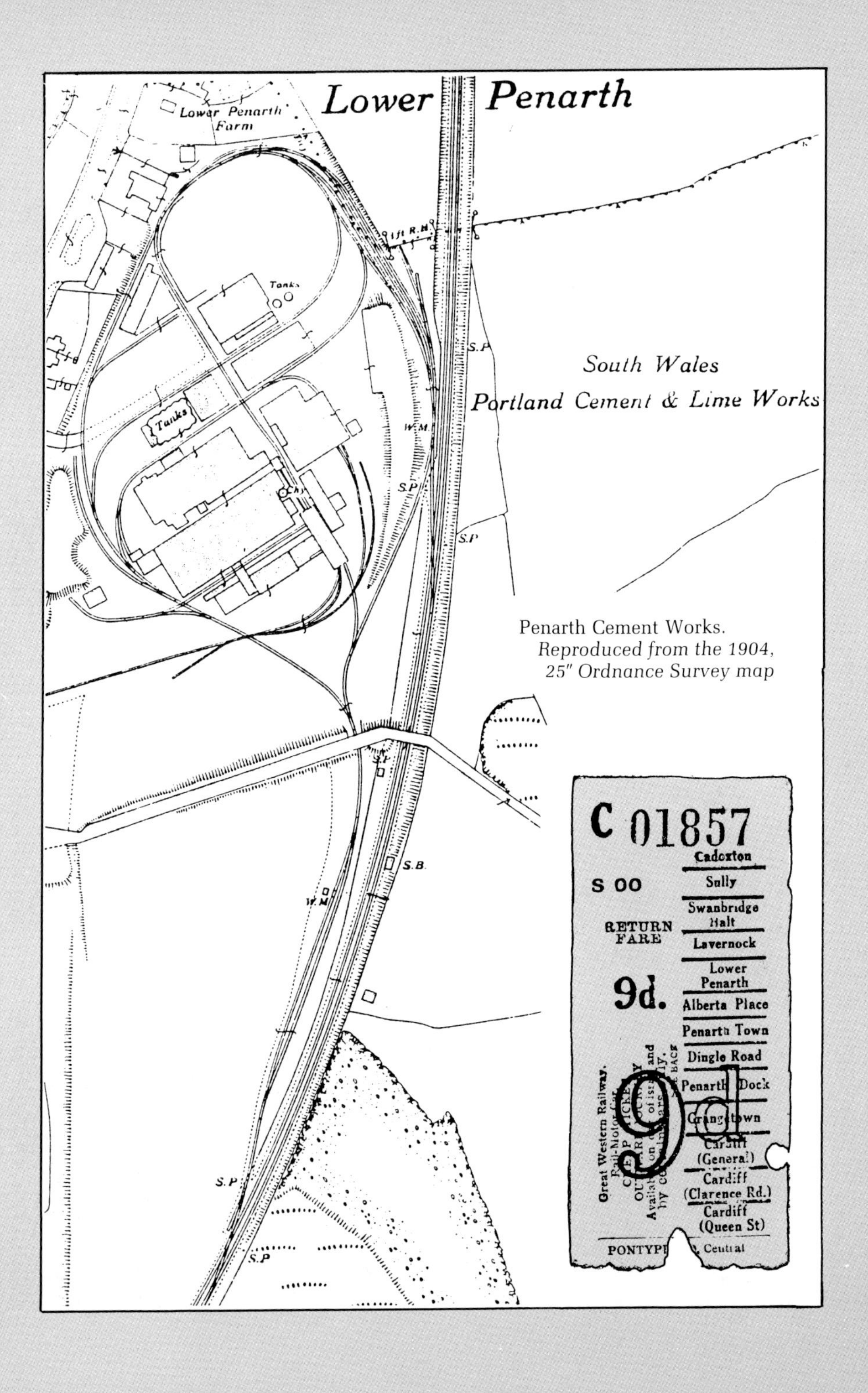

Penarth Cement Works.
Reproduced from the 1904, 25" Ordnance Survey map

The last day of the service was Saturday 4th May, 1968. The final train is recorded as a three-car diesel multiple unit which left Penarth 17 minutes late at 11.44 pm carrying 17 passengers, with little interest shown by the local population.

For the previous 15 months most Cadoxton services had been operated by a single-car diesel unit, and staff had been withdrawn from stations, tickets being issued on the trains.

After withdrawal of the Cadoxton passenger trains, a single track remained in position between Penarth Town and the cement works at Lower Penarth, stop blocks being erected at about 2 miles 60 chains (measured from Cogan Junction). The signals and signal boxes at Penarth Town and the Cement Works were taken out of use, and a hand-operated run-round loop provided at the Cement Works. The connection at Penarth Town onto the Cement Works line continued to be controlled from a ground frame. At about this time the sidings and goods shed at Penarth were removed.

A freight train generally ran to and from the Cement Works three times per week, but this ceased with the closure of the works in November 1969, when the line beyond Penarth Town closed, and the track 'layout' at Penarth became what it is today, a single track with stop blocks at the end of a 1 mile 11 chains branch from Cogan Junction. The down platform buildings, including canopy, were adapted for the use of a commercial firm and remained until 1990, when they were replaced by a larger building, the premises of which encroach onto where the down line used to be.

The Transport Act of 1968 first established the principle of Government grants for loss-making passenger services which were considered desirable for social or economic reasons, and the Penarth line has been supported in this way since 1st January, 1969. For the first six years, grants were awarded to specific train services, rather than on the national network-wide basis of the Public Service Obligation Grant that has applied since the Railways Act of 1974. The grant for the Cardiff–Penarth service for each of the first two years, 1969 and 1970, was set at £63,000.

To reduce costs, 'conductor guard working' was introduced, as on other local services radiating from Cardiff, on 2nd February, 1970, resulting in tickets being issued on trains, with station ticket offices manned only at busy times. Changes to station facilities ensued, with a brick waiting shelter incorporating a simple ticket office being provided at Dingle Road. Later, in 1974, the 'up side' TVR station building in use at Penarth was replaced by a simpler brick structure containing booking office, booking hall and waiting shelter – brought into use on 23rd December, 1974 – and a second brick shelter was provided at Dingle Road. The 1974 works were supported by a Welsh Office Capital Grant under Section 56 of the 1968 Transport Act.

A useful barometer of passenger traffic at about this time are BR figures for 1973 showing daily averages of 675, 429 and 231 passengers joining trains at Penarth, Dingle Road and Grangetown respectively, reducing on Saturdays to averages of 571, 261 and 125 respectively. Fares from Penarth to Cardiff at this time were 85p (weekly season), 20p (ordinary return), 18p (cheap day return) and 11p (single).

A view of Alberta Place, looking towards Penarth, taken on 4th August, 1969, after the passenger service had been withdrawn fifteen months beforehand, but while a single track was still in place for freight trains running to and from the cement works at Lower Penarth. *I.L. Wright*

The exterior of the brick 'vandalproof' building at Penarth station, photographed eight months after being brought into use in December 1974. Beyond (*right*) is the tiled roof and chimneys of the former down side building, then in commercial use. *British Rail*

The brick shelters on the remaining (former up) platform at Dingle Road, photographed looking towards Penarth in July 1978. A ticket office, with a window close to the gate, is incorporated in the nearer building.
British Rail

A Penarth-bound three-car class '116' dmu at Dingle Road in July 1978. The train is in the short-lived white livery with blue band introduced when these dmu sets were refurbished from 1976 onwards. The former down platform can be seen to the right. *British Rail*

PENARTH TO CARDIFF PENARTH TO CARDIFF

Your local line Your local line

EXTRA TRAINS ON THE PENARTH LINE

From February 20 to March 17.

Journey time 11 minutes

50p DAY RETURN

Valid for travel Monday to Friday by any train on or after 0900 Saturday or Sunday by any train.

£2.80 5 DAY WEEKLY SEASON

HERE IS THE FULL TIMETABLE: Until 13 May 1984 | Extra trains. If successful they may become permanent later in 1984.

		SX							
Penarth	d	0535	0608	0653	0730	0800	0836	0900	0930
Dingle Road	d	0537	0610	0655	0732	0802	0838	0902	0932
Grangetown	d	0542	0615	0700	0737	0807	0843	0907	0937
Central	a	0546	0619	0704	0741	0811	0847	0911	0941
Queen Street	a		0623	0708	0745	0816	0850	0916	0945
Penarth	d	**0950**	1030	**1050**	1130	**1150**	1230	**1250**	1330
Dingle Road	d	**0952**	1032	**1052**	1132	**1152**	1232	**1252**	1332
Grangetown	d	**0957**	1037	**1057**	1137	**1157**	1237	**1257**	1337
Central	a	**1001**	1041	**1101**	1141	**1201**	1241	**1301**	1341
Queen Street	a	**1005**	1045	**1105**	1145	**1205**	1245	**1307**	1345
Penarth	d	**1350**	1430	**1450**	1530	**1550**	1630	**1645**	1713
Dingle Road	d	**1352**	1432	**1452**	1532	**1552**	1632	**1647**	1715
Grangetown	d	**1357**	1437	**1457**	1537	**1557**	1637	**1652**	1720
Central	a	**1401**	1441	**1501**	1541	**1601**	1641	**1656**	1726
Queen Street	a	**1405b**	1445	**1505**	1545	**1605**	1645	**1705c**	1729
Penarth	d	1738	1806	1909	2010	2115	2220	2308	
Dingle Road	d	1740	1808	1911	2012	2117	2222	2310	
Grangetown	d	1745	1813	1916	2017	2122	2227	2315	
Central	a	1749	1817	1920	2021	2126	2231	2319	
Queen Street	a	1754	1834			2130	2236	2325	
SUNDAYS									
Penarth	d	0750	0950	1218	1350	1710	1858	2215	
Dingle Road	d	0752	0952	1220	1352	1712	1900	2217	
Grangetown	a	0757	0957	1225	1357	1717	1905	2222	
Central	a	0801	1001	1229	1401	1721	1909	2226	

						SX	SO	SX	SO
Queen Street	d		0632	0708	0737	0808	0746e	0832	0825e
Central	d	0543	0636	0712	0742	0812	0812	0836	0836
Grangetown	d	0547	0640	0716	0746	0816	0816	0840	0840
Dingle Road	a	0552	0645	0721	0751	0821	0821	0845	0845
Penarth	a	0554	0647	0723	0753	0823	0823	0847	0847
Queen Street	d	0907	**0925**	0944	**1025**	1044	**1125**	1144	**1225**
Central	d	0911	**0929**	0948	**1029**	1048	**1129**	1151	**1229**
Grangetown	d	0915	**0933**	0952	**1033**	1052	**1133**	1155	**1233**
Dingle Road	a	0920	**0938**	0957	**1038**	1057	**1138**	1200	**1238**
Penarth	a	0922	**0940**	0959	**1040**	1059	**1140**	1202	**1240**
Queen Street	d	1244	**1325**	1344	**1425**	1444	**1525**	1607	**1625**
Central	d	1248	**1329**	1351	**1429**	1448	**1529**	1611	**1629**
Grangetown	d	1252	**1333**	1355	**1433**	1452	**1533**	1615	**1633**
Dingle Road	a	1257	**1338**	1400	**1438**	1457	**1538**	1620	**1638**
Penarth	a	1259	**1340**	1402	**1440**	1459	**1540**	1622	**1640**
Queen Street	d	1648	1715	1747	1844	1929	2053	2158	2238
Central	d	1652	1720	1751	1853	1933	2057	2202	2242
Grangetown	d	1656	1724	1755	1857	1937	2101	2206	2246
Dingle Road	a	1701	1729	1800	1902	1942	2106	2211	2251
Penarth	a	1703	1731	1802	1904	1944	2108	2213	2253
SUNDAYS									
Central	d	0725	0935	1200	1320	1655	1826	2140	
Grangetown	d	0729	0939	1204	1324	1659	1830	2144	
Dingle Road	a	0734	0944	1209	1329	1704	1835	2149	
Penarth	a	0736	0946	1211	1331	1706	1837	2151	

NOTES SX Saturdays excepted. SO Saturdays only. b Saturdays only. c Saturdays arrive 1709. e Change Cardiff Central

A folder issued by British Rail in 1984 featuring the experimental two-trains-per-hour off-peak weekday train service on the Penarth line. The additional trains were so successful that they became permanent, and led to increased frequencies in due course throughout the Valley Lines network.

At Grangetown the platform buildings were replaced by a simple brick wind-break with seating, positioned beneath the metal canopy which was left in position. Briefly taking the story ahead into the next decade, the canopy was taken down in the Autumn of 1983, and the wind-break was enlarged to a twin-sided brick shelter. Later, to brighten the surroundings generally, South Glamorgan County Council commissioned a sculpture with a railway theme in the stairway leading up from the road to the station, and provided walled flower beds on the platform. These improvements were officially inaugurated on Saturday 22nd September, 1984 by the Rt Hon. James Callaghan, the local MP and former Prime Minister.

The County Councils set up under local government re-organisation in 1974 have a responsibility for transport planning. South Glamorgan, together with Mid Glamorgan, displayed from the start considerable support for the local passenger train services centred on Cardiff. While long-term options were studied, this support first found fruit in the 'park and ride' car parks at certain stations, including Cogan, on the Barry line, but within the Penarth town boundary.

County Council funding of new stations began with Cathays, north of Cardiff Queen Street on the Taff main line and opened on 3rd October, 1983. Concurrently the new Provincial Services business sector management ('Regional Railways' since December 1990) on British Rail resulted in a more positive and imaginative management attitude towards rural and suburban passenger train services, and a new BR marketing campaign began with the reduction of many local fares in the Cardiff area as from 9th October, 1983. On the Penarth line the day ticket fares were reduced by roughly 33 per cent, and season tickets by about 15 per cent.

These measures arrested a decline in traffic and led to more passengers on the Penarth line, but not in sufficient numbers to increase overall revenue to BR. To see, therefore, whether revenue would increase if more trains were provided, the Penarth line was chosen for an experimental two-trains-per-hour off-peak service as from 20th February, 1984. Its success in increasing passenger *and* revenue levels was such that it became a permanent feature of the timetable, and service frequencies were similarly stepped up on other parts of the local Cardiff network. This network was, incidentally, known officially by the term 'Valley Lines' as from 2nd February, 1985.

The Mid and South Glamorgan County Councils published a supportive, forward-looking 'Cardiff Valleys Rail Development Strategy' in September, 1985, and on the combined initiatives of BR and the Counties, the Valley Lines witnessed a thorough revolution as from 5th October, 1987. On the Penarth line this involved a three-trains-per-hour, roughly 20 minutes frequency, timetable throughout most of the day, with the majority of services operated by the new 'Sprinter' diesel trains. Penarth trains continued to run through from and to points on the Valley Lines north of Cardiff including, from October the following year, the re-opened Aberdare line.

The most dramatic change in October, 1987 occurred, however, on the northern section of the PHDR line, between Radyr and Ninian Park.

Before coming to this, the recent history of Ninian Park requires clarification. After World War II the platforms were again used for football traffic,

Ninian Park station in June 1983, when used (as since 1912) only for football traffic and other special events. The view is towards Penarth Curve North Junction, where the PHDR line to Penarth continues ahead, with the route to Cardiff Central diverging to the left. The BR Canton depot is also on the left, with the stands of Cardiff City Football Club's ground to the right. *D.W. Lewis*

Diesel-electric locomotive No. 45 070 passing the site of the present day Danescourt station *en route* to Radyr with the empty stock of a special excursion train which it had brought into Ninian Park on 2nd June, 1982, in connection with the visit to Cardiff of H.H. Pope John Paul. *D.J. Morgan*

The official inauguration of construction work on City Line stations in 1987, with pavoir blocks being laid at Ninian Park station by Councillor Gordon Houlston, Chairman of South Glamorgan County Council (*right*) and John Pearse, BR's Western Provincial Services Manager (*left*). Looking on in the background are BR Officers (*left to right*) John Davies, Hugh Gould (Manager, Wales) and Ken King. *D.W. Lewis*

The 10.32 am Merthyr Tydfil to Cardiff Central, formed of three-car class '116' dmu set C.320 and at the time the only regular passenger train routed over the Radyr–Ninian Park section of the PHDR line (and running non-stop from Treforest), passes construction work at the future Danescourt station in August 1987. *D.J. Morgan*

BR 'City Line' and South Glamorgan County Council 'Countyride' insignia at the entrance to Tyllgoed/Fairwater station. The Welsh version of the station name is in green lettering, the English in black, as is standard on BR bilingual signs. 'Countyride' denotes a public transport facility financed by the County Council. Another sign at the station entrance announces the support received from the European Regional Development Fund. *N.W. Sprinks*

Guard Stephen Wake and Driver Claud Old at Cardiff Central on Sunday, 4th October, 1987, prior to taking 'Sprinter' No. 150261 as the 06.26 service to Merthyr Tydfil, the first passenger carrying train of the new 'City Line' service over the PHDR route to Radyr which began that day. As explained in *Chapter 2*, a dress rehearsal of the new weekday timetable was carried out on this day prior to introduction on Monday, 5th October, 1987. *D.W. Lewis*

although there are reports that in August 1952 the pre-war Sunday St Fagans–Barry excursions were revived, routed via Leckwith Junction and calling at Ninian Park, then going on via Penarth. However, Ninian Park was closed from 1st November, 1974 to 29th January, 1977 (apart from 4th October, 1975), due to vandalism, during which time the Pagoda shelter, along with anything else removable, was taken away. It was also used on the occasion of the visit to Cardiff of H.H. Pope John Paul II on Wednesday 2nd June, 1982, undoubtedly the busiest day in its history. Apart from excursions from the valleys and other parts of South Wales and Bristol, long distance trains from Manchester (2), Portsmouth, Retford, Basingstoke and Rock Ferry all arrived at, and departed from Ninian Park Platform. One oddity was that whilst other Taff Vale Railmotor platforms were renamed halts by the GWR in 1922, Ninian Park retained the 'platform' status throughout GWR days, in fact it is only in very recent years that, officially, it seems to have dropped the suffix altogether.

From 5th October, 1987 Ninian Park has seen, however, a regular train service as part of the South Glamorgan County Council-funded 'City Line' scheme, which embraced the provision of stations on the Radyr–Ninian Park section, and the upgrading of stations on the ex-Cardiff Railway line to Coryton (and, on the Coryton section, a new station at Ty Glas). The City Line concept was a through Radyr–Cardiff–Coryton service at a minimum middle-day off-peak frequency of 30 minutes, although for the first two years the service was provided mainly by trains which, north of Radyr, originated at or ran to Taffs Well or Merthyr Tydfil.

The Radyr–Ninian Park–Cardiff Central line, after a period of over 128 years as a freight carrying railway, with just occasional use for special or diverted passenger trains, thus became a regular passenger carrying railway for the first time: although for accuracy's sake it must be mentioned that since 13th May, 1985 the line had been used by one morning train from Merthyr Tydfil each weekday in order to run into the 'up' main line side of Cardiff Central to make connections. Indeed, for the first 12 months, this train ran through to Bristol.

The stations between Radyr and Cardiff Central are at Danescourt, Fairwater/Tyllgoed (just south of the erstwhile Waterhall Junction), Waun-gron Park and Ninian Park. The County Council spent £692,000, partly funded by a European Regional Development Fund grant, on the provision of the first three stations, and the refurbishing of Ninian Park. At Danescourt, Fairwater and Waun-gron Park new platforms were provided, each of two-car 'Sprinter' length, with lighting, shelters and access, while at Danescourt and Fairwater footbridges were necessary as well. Similar amenities were provided on a sufficiently long section of Ninian Park's two platforms, although BR has refurbished the full length of the down platform for departing football specials.

Although the new Valley Lines and City Line service officially began on Monday 5th October, 1987, the full weekday service operated the previous day, Sunday, as training for staff and as an introduction for passengers who had the benefit of the freedom of the Valley Lines for the day for just 50p.

Two-car 'Sprinter' dmus No. 150280 (*left*, on a Coryton–Taffs Well service) and No. 150277 (*right*, *en route* from Merthyr Tydfil to Coryton) at Fairwater on 6th October, 1987, during the first week of 'City Line' operation. *D.W. Lewis*

A Merthyr to Coryton 'Sprinter' dmu in the first week of City Line operation in October 1987 passing construction work at Waun-gron Park station which, for reasons explained opposite, opened four weeks later than the other new City Line stations. *D.W. Lewis*

Due to difficulties in constructing Waun-gron Park station on an embankment and rail-over-road bridge, its opening was delayed for four weeks until Monday 2nd November, 1987, with an official opening four days later involving Wyn (now Sir Wyn) Roberts, M.P., Minister of State at the Welsh Office.

The Radyr–Cardiff Central section of the City Line was introduced under the provisions of the 'Speller Act', i.e. a new Section 56A added in 1981 to the Transport Act of 1962, whereby train services can be introduced on an experimental basis, and, if found unsuccessful, the services can be withdrawn without going through the normal lengthy closure-of-lines procedure. Being experimental, the service is not entitled to financial support from the Government Public Service Obligation Grant, as received by the rest of the Valley Lines network, and all BR costs have to be met from income. It should be explained that although the County Council has made capital investment in the service, it does not provide revenue support towards the service's on-going costs.

1987 also saw developments at Penarth. The County Council provided at a cost of £5,000 an additional waiting shelter which also includes access and a cycle rack, while BR refurbished and improved the 1974 station building.

Notable at the start of 1987 was South Glamorgan County Council's long term proposal to restore ¾-mile of the Penarth–Cadoxton line, to a proposed station just short of the Forrest Road bridge, between the former Alberta Place and Lower Penarth halts. The plan, which would have cost the Council £355,000 at then current prices, had the support of BR who estimated that some 200 extra passengers would use the Penarth line each weekday, attracted by the new station situated close to housing developments.

The exterior of Penarth station on 19th August, 1991. Of note is the bus stop sign for route P.11 to Lower Penarth introduced in 1987 when plans for the extension of the line to Lower Penarth were rejected by the local population; and the additional 'Countyride' entrance, waiting shelter and cycle park provided by South Glamorgan County Council. *N.W. Sprinks*

The down side canopy and buildings at Penarth being dismantled in February 1990, 23 years after they had ceased to be used by passengers and during which time the premises had been in commercial use. A Sprinter dmu is at the former up platform waiting to depart for Cardiff and beyond. *D.W. Lewis*

Two-car 'Sprinter' dmu No. 150278 waiting to leave Penarth as the 15.25 service to Treherbert on 19th August, 1991. On the right is the new commercial building which in 1990 replaced the former down side station premises. *N.W. Sprinks*

Some enlightened voices pointed out that the extension would reduce traffic on the roads, and improve the finances, and therefore security, of the whole Penarth line. However, there were many objections from local residents on the grounds of loss of amenities and because they feared increased disturbance, traffic and on-street parking, in addition to a loss of property values, in the vicinity of the proposed station.

The interim solution which had been in the Council's mind was therefore introduced, and the rail scheme abandoned, later in the year. The interim proposal was a feeder bus service from Lower Penarth to Penarth station in the morning, with a similar return service in the evenings, and this began on 26th October, 1987, subsidised by the County Council. At the time of writing (1992) there are four 'hail-and-ride' journeys each Monday to Friday morning starting from Cosmeston Estate, which is on the site of the erstwhile cement works. Four journeys also apply in the evening, connecting with train arrivals from Cardiff. The bus route is numbered P11.

It is interesting to compare the passenger train services over the different sections of the Taff Vale lines to Penarth that have applied under three different ownerships and at intervals of forty-plus years:

NUMBER OF TRAINS IN EACH DIRECTION PER DAY (MONDAYS TO FRIDAYS)

	TVR 1905	*GWR 1947*	*BR 1992*
Radyr to Ninian Park (Cardiff Central)	–	–	28
Penarth to Cardiff	42	38	42
Barry to Cardiff (over PHDR through Grangetown)	27*	31	47
Cadoxton to Penarth	13	13	–
TOTALS	82	82	117

*Operated by Barry Railway.

For historical record it is appropriate to record some fares from the current decade. In a fares revision effective from 30th September, 1990, the 7-day season ticket price from Radyr, Danescourt, Fairwater, Waun-gron Park, Penarth or Dingle Road to Cardiff (Central, Queen Street, Bute Road and Cathays stations) was £6.40, with a day return fare of £1.60, and a 'low' (off-peak) day return fare of £1. The single fare was also £1.

Since the 1960s the amount of freight carried by rail has steadily reduced through the emergence of the national motorway network and ever increasing lorry sizes. Coupled with this there have been dramatic industrial changes, particularly affecting the heavy industries of coal and steel on which South Wales had traditionally relied. At the same time, the railways have concentrated on their competitive strength of moving large quantities

The Tower Colliery (Hirwaun) to Aberthaw Power Station 'Merry-Go-Round' coal trains alone perpetuate the original coal carrying purpose of the PHDR, and traverse the line throughout from Radyr to Cogan Junction, then continuing over the ex-Barry Railway. This recent photograph of the one of these trains, passing over the Penarth Curve North to Penarth Curve South Junctions section, shows 1,750 h.p. diesel-electric locomotive No. 37 899 *County of West Glamorgan/Sir Gorllewin Morgannwg*, in Trainload Coal livery, hauling the customary 28-wagon load. In the background is Canton depot. *D.W. Lewis*

New 3,100 h.p. diesel-electric locomotive No. 60 023 *The Cheviot* passing Fairwater in November 1990, hauling empty container wagons *en route* from Cardiff Cathays Works, via Radyr. *B. Rolley*

of freight in bulk train loads. The result of all these changes is that freight moved by rail in the Valleys of Mid Glamorgan is now only coal, deep mined or opencast, and this has reduced with the rapid contraction of the deep mining of coal in the Taff, Cynon and Rhondda valleys in the 1980s and the cessation of patent fuel manufacture at Abercwmboi, near Aberdare.

There has, therefore, been a sharp decline in freight traffic through Radyr and over the Radyr–Penarth Curves section of the PHDR. This was also accentuated by the closure in June, 1982 of the Aber Junction–Taffs Well freight line and the consequent routeing via Caerphilly and Cardiff Queen Street of all coal trains from the former Rhymney Railway line.

Today the most notable freight trains over the PHDR are the 'merry-go-round' coal trains from Tower colliery, near Hirwaun in the upper Cynon Valley, to Aberthaw Power Station. These traverse the PHDR throughout from Radyr to Cogan Junction.

Since July 1990 Radyr yard has served mainly as a stabling point for rolling stock being repaired at BR or private workshops in the Cardiff area, notably the BR (ex-TVR) works at Cathays, and the PHDR route provides a convenient route from and to the South Wales main line, via Penarth Curve North Junction. Radyr yard also incorporates a BR track pre-assembly depot which generates considerable traffic in engineering department trains.

The Penarth Curve South Junction–Cogan Junction section of the PHDR sees, in addition to the Penarth passenger trains, the equally frequent – sometimes more so – passenger service to and from Barry Island, together with freight trains of which the 'merry-go-round' coal trains to Aberthaw are the most frequent. Also bound for the Barry line are freight trains to and from installations on Barry Docks, trains moving wagons for repair at the BR workshops at Barry, trains to and from Aberthaw cement works, and to and from the Ford Engine Plant at Bridgend which is reached by a spur opened in 1980 off the Barry–Bridgend 'Vale of Glamorgan' line.

On the Ely Tidal Harbour line, after the cessation of coal traffic at the end of 1962, there were still a couple of oil companies and private firms connected to the branch. The Esso sidings were taken out of use in 1981, and the last ½-mile of the branch fell into disuse after April of that year, but was not officially cut back to 1 mile 78 chains until 1st August, 1983. The branch is still (early 1992) connected to the former BP Oil Company depot and the Taff Wagon Works site, and the most recent traffic has been tank cars for BP, but since the last movement of these in the Winter 1989/90 the line has been out of use, and is likely to be taken up in due course unless some new traffic materialises. There is a long run-round loop at the Grangetown end and the line, single track, has been cut short at the Ferry Road BP terminal, some 62 chains from Grangetown Junction.

The signalling on all the lines described in this book is, at the present time, by colour lights controlled from the Cardiff 'Panel' box. This is with the exception of the Radyr area, however, where GWR-type semaphore signals survive, some controlled from a TVR-built signal box at Radyr Quarry, alongside the PHDR line, which serves as a convenient and visible reminder of the line's former ownership.

The disused Ferry Road BP Oil Terminal, also the present terminating point of the disused line towards Ely Tidal Harbour, photographed in August 1991. *N.W. Sprinks*

Two-car 'Sprinter' dmu No. 150244 working the 10.47 Treherbert to Penarth service on 21st August, 1991, immediately after traversing Cogan Junction, with the Barry line curving away to the left. The new road bridge immediately behind the train crosses the railway and the river Ely, on the farther bank of which can be seen some of the decaying wharves of the former Ely Tidal Harbour. *N.W. Sprinks*

A survey of the Taff Vale lines to Penarth would be incomplete without some reference to the transformation in recent years at Penarth Dock which, for many years, was the foremost *raison d'etre* of the railway. Some of the dock estate now sees light industrial activity, but the basin and remaining dock have blossomed into new life as the Portway Yacht Marina, complete with waterside housing. New lock gates have been fitted. Now there are proposals for further housing and leisure facilities, together with shops, offices, a boat yard and light industry in 56 acres of the filled-in area of the dock, to be known as Penarth Haven. The area generally falls within that being regenerated by the Cardiff Bay Development Corporation, set up in 1987, whose plans include a ¾-mile barrage across the mouths of the rivers Ely and Taff, linking Cardiff's Queen Alexandra Dock with Penarth Head. A Bill is currently (1992) passing through Parliament. The Corporation's plans for the erstwhile Ely Tidal Harbour and adjacent land provide for mixed use waterside development, including housing, commerce, leisure and park-land.

Attempting an assessment, as this book closes for press, of the present situation on the lines which were formerly the Penarth Harbour, Dock and Railway and the Penarth Extension Railway, and daring a look into the future, there is little doubt that the movement of passengers is looked upon as their most important role at the present time. Indeed in many quarters an expanding role is seen for these railway lines – and others in the region – for the future, so that their carrying capacity is increased, and so easing the ever growing road traffic problems in the Cardiff area and even avoiding the need for costly road improvement schemes.

In stressing the passenger role, the freight traffic over the Radyr–Penarth Curves–Cogan Junction sections of the PHDR is not overlooked: and depending on industrial developments, on national policies in relation to the movement of freight by rail, and the potential for the Channel Tunnel to increase the proportion of international freight carried by rail in Britain, freight trains should continue to be part of the scene on these sections of line.

When passenger services began in 1987 on the Radyr–Ninian Park section of the PHDR, the County Council hoped that the new stations would generate some 1,000 passenger journeys each day, but reports suggest that the actual number of journeys has settled around the 800 mark. As the train service is experimental, all BR's costs have to be covered from income. Despite this difficulty, the South Glamorgan County Council appear anxious to protect their investment in the new stations, and that the service should continue to play its part in encouraging people to use public transport and so ease road congestion. Measures are accordingly constantly under review with Regional Railways with a view to making the service more attractive and reliable and at the same time to reduce costs. The recent introduction of the 'Pacer' trains – referred to in more detail in the next chapter – is part of this process: while the County Council is in fact purchasing the one 'Pacer' unit allocated for accountancy purposes to the Radyr–Ninian Park–Cardiff Central service, so that the interest and depreciation charges for the unit are borne by the County Council instead of BR, facilitating BR's obligation to

The Customs House at Penarth Dock, fenced-off, bricked-up and awaiting restoration, photographed in August 1991. The building is engraved 'Erected A.D. 1865', the year in which Penarth Dock was opened. *N.W. Sprinks*

An August 1991 view of the Portway Village Marina now established in the former Penarth Dock. *N.W. Sprinks*

match its costs with income from fares. A hindrance to timetabling and reliability is the section of single track between Ninian Park and Cardiff Central, over the 22 chains of the Penarth Curve North to East Junctions spur.

Another factor in the future is found in the plans now being studied and publicly debated, for the capacity of the train service from the Taff Valley to Cardiff to be significantly developed and increased, as an alternative to expensive proposals for increasing the capacity of the parallel A470 trunk road. If these plans materialise into an increased frequency of train service from Pontypridd, etc., there is little doubt that the routeing of some trains over the PHDR Radyr–Ninian Park approach to Cardiff would be necessary, to avoid overloading the Taff main line via Llandaff and its busy junction at Queen Street with the Rhymney and Coryton lines.

As an aside to this, it is interesting to note that with the restoration of a Cardiff–Bridgend–Maesteg passenger train service as from 28th September, 1992 – for which the initial capital costs were funded by Mid Glamorgan County Council and the European Regional Development Fund (as with the Aberdare passenger re-opening four years previously) – some of the trains are scheduled out of and into Cardiff Central via the Leckwith loop. They thus traverse Penarth Curve East and North Junctions, the PHDR line through Ninian Park station, and then the Leckwith loop connection with the South Wales main line. This is the first regular passenger service over the 1932 Leckwith loop.

Over the PHDR route from Penarth Curve South Junction through Grangetown to Cogan Junction, the Valley Lines passenger services between Cardiff and Barry and Penarth are very well established, particularly since the service and marketing improvements of the mid-1980s and the subsequent introduction of modern trains, all of which have been described earlier in this chapter. The Penarth trains continue, of course, over the erstwhile Penarth Extension Railway to Dingle Road and Penarth stations.

The plans of the Cardiff Bay Development Corporation frequently refer to the possibility of a 'light rail' public transport network within its area: 'light rail' embraces systems such as the new 'Metrolink Super Tram' service in Manchester, running partly over former BR lines, and partly in city streets. What form a Cardiff Bay 'light rail' system would take, what its network would be, and whether it would be integrated in any way with BR Regional Railways lines (known for comparative purposes as 'heavy rail'), appear subject to debate, and will be for future recorders of the railway scene to relate.

It must also be for future historians to record whether 'light rail' eventually extends across the Taff and Ely rivers to Penarth – perhaps over the proposed Barrage – and whether, in these circumstances, this has any effect on the future of the BR Regional Railways line to Penarth. At present this line serves Penarthians well as it has done since 1878, and it would be satisfying if this tradition were to continue.

The story of the Taff Vale Railway's lines to Penarth is far from over!

The 9.13 am Penarth Town to Cardiff (Clarence Road) train, propelled by ex-GWR 0–6–0PT No. 6435, at Penarth Dock station on 20th October, 1958. *R.O. Tuck*

Chapter Three

Locomotive and Train Working

Of the three Penarth railways dealt with only the PHDR ever possessed any locomotives of its own, the other two companies being worked entirely by the TVR from their commencement. Even the PHDR only worked its coal traffic, between the main line junction at Radyr and Penarth Harbour, for the short period until the Taff took over in 1863. The small company had three engines, two 0–6–0 tender engines which were pretty standard for coal traffic in those early days, along with a 2–4–0 tender engine. The latter was a strange choice as 2–4–0s were almost as standard for passenger work, but passenger trains were certainly not envisaged by the Penarth company. As it had comparatively small driving wheels for a 2–4–0, of 4 ft 6 in. diameter, it was thus reasonably suitable for mineral working. And as no severe gradients were involved, that may well be the reason it was acquired, particularly if it was spare on the maker's hands, and obtainable fairly cheaply compared with the much sought after 0–6–0s.

There is no record whether the Penarth company erected a small shed for its locos, but if it did it was likely to have been near the junction at Radyr. Certainly the Taff erected one in 1865 almost alongside the junction, which, for the remainder of the TVR's independent existence, always held a large number of 0–6–0 tender engines, no less than 17 still being shedded there in 1922 when the GWR took control. In the early days the tonnage shipped at the Harbour (in 1863) was only 182,620, some 3,500 tons per week, hence one engine would have been sufficient to take the traffic from the junction to the Harbour; probably another was used at the latter place to push the wagons to the coal tips.

The first class of tank engines, eight 0–6–0STs, did not appear on the Taff until 1865/7. At that time the company preferred the tender engines because of the extra brake power coming down the severe gradients on many sections of the line. Initially the tank engines were used as bankers towards the northern section, but as more powerful engines were built, the tank engines were transferred to pilot duties, and a couple almost certainly were used as Penarth Dock pilots from the early/mid-1870s.

By the 1880s the steam coal export trade was increasing at an astonishing rate, and a number of storage sidings were laid down at convenient sites to the docks to enable train loads of coal to be berthed until the ship was available and ready to take the particular load. The storage sidings for Penarth Docks were at Llandough, a comparatively short distance from the junctions to the dock sidings. A much larger yard was laid out at Radyr, alongside the Penarth line, which also had the capacity to cater for trains of empty wagons returning to the collieries. By that time the two 0–6–0STs formerly used for transferring the coal traffic to the tips, were relegated to works and yard shunting mainly at Cardiff, and Penarth was allotted two of the very powerful 0–6–0Ts of the four purchased second-hand from the Metropolitan Railway.

At much the same time Penarth had become the principal southern terminus for TVR passenger trains, hence the need for a locomotive shed to cater for passenger, mineral and shunting engines. To avoid too many light engine

TVR 'L' Class 0–6–0 freight locomotive No. 6. *The National Museum of Wales*

TVR 0–6–0T No. 91, one of four purchased second-hand from the Metropolitan Railway in 1868 and 1875. Two of these locomotives were allocated to Penarth Dock shed. *The National Museum of Wales*

TVR '0.4' Class 0–6–2T No. 39, one of a class introduced between 1907 and 1910. *Oakwood Press Collection*

movements, the shed was erected alongside Penarth Dock station and opened in 1887. Although this still involved a few 'passenger' light engine movements up the 1 in 40 bank between Penarth Dock and Penarth Town station, these were few compared with the far more numerous movements involved with mineral and shunting engines, had the shed been sited near the Town station. Certainly passenger train facilities existed at Penarth Town, as when the service started carriage sidings, a carriage shed, a locomotive turntable and – possibly – a small engine shed had been provided close to the station. However the carriage shed burned down on 7th July, 1884 destroying 10 carriages, and after that date only siding accommodation, the turntable, and water facilities survived. By that time Penarth had become a select residential area with a modest sea front, the docks – and the new engine shed – being hidden from view by Penarth Head, which was doubtless appreciated by the residents, and may have had some bearing on the siting of the new shed.

By the mid-1890s, 0–6–2 tank engines had started to replace the 0–6–0 tender engines on mineral traffic, although this was not to any appreciable extent until the advent of the powerful 'O4' class in the early 1900s. For passenger work a variety of engines had been used, first 2–4–0 tender engines, followed in 1884 by 4–4–0 outside cylinder tank engines, and then in 1888 by 4–4–2 inside cylinder tank engines. However in the mid/late-1890s the principal passenger workings were taken over by the 'U' and 'U1' classes of 0–6–2Ts. These had 5 ft 3 in. diameter driving wheels and were popularly known as the 'High Flyers'. The ex-Metropolitan tank engines on the storage sidings to tip workings were replaced in 1899, by the powerful 'V' class 0–6–0STs, which Mr Tom Hurry Riches had especially designed for such work. Thus Penarth shed, at the turn of the century had about six of the passenger 0–6–2Ts, about an equal number of mineral 0–6–2Ts, some four or five of the old 0–6–0 mineral tender engines, together with three or four dock shunters – a total allocation of around 20 or 21 engines.

There was plenty of interest in the carriage stock using the Penarth section. Whilst some of the earlier four-wheeled carriage stock was used when the Penarth to Cardiff section was isolated from the TVR main line, once through running was achieved in 1883 most trains were composed of more modern four-wheeled stock, from the large batch constructed by the Metropolitan Railway Carriage and Wagon Co in 1873/4. Several of these, listed below, were destroyed in the fire at Penarth Carriage Shed already referred to:

2 – 4 wheel 2nd/3rd Composites
4 – 6 wheel 1st/2nd Composites
1 – Brake Composite 1st/2nd/Guard
2 – Brake Thirds
1 – Third

Replacement carriages were quickly ordered from the Metropolitan Company, but the carriage shed at Penarth was never rebuilt. In February 1885 two close-coupled 'block' trains were ordered from the Oldbury Carriage Co. each train consisting of seven vehicles, for use on the Penarth line. A year

TVR 2–4–0 passenger locomotive No. 33, built in 1874, as rebuilt in 1885.
Oakwood Press Collection

TVR 'I' Class 4–4–0T No. 67, one of a class of three locomotives, all built in 1884/5. They were later fitted for auto working, and later still fitted with larger boilers. Before being adapted for auto working the locomotives, numbered Nos. 67, 68 and 69, were renumbered Nos. 285, 286 and 287. *The National Museum of Wales*

TVR 'U.1' Class 0–6–2T passenger locomotive No. 30, photographed at Penarth Town. The seven locomotives of this class were delivered in 1896.
Oakwood Press Collection

later the Metropolitan Company supplied two close-coupled 1st/2nd Composite coaches, one for each of the 'block' trains. These had a second class compartment at each end, but the intended two firsts in the centre were opened out into saloons, with one door on each side diagonally placed, so that the remainder of the sides and ends could comprise continuous seating around a card table fixed centrally. As such the two carriages were known as the Club Cars, and were only used in the mornings and late afternoons to convey important businessmen from their homes at Penarth to the heart of Cardiff's dockland and back again. The train in which they were formed was known as the Penarth Clubman's train. With a journey of only some 15 to 18 minutes the 'clubman' must have been hard pressed to get through many decks of cards!

The carriages which formed the main line trains from the heads of the valleys and which terminated at Penarth, comprised eight-wheeled stock by the mid-1880s, although there was always a six-wheeled passenger brake van at each end. Many of the eight-wheeled coaches constructed in the 1880s were non-bogie vehicles, generally known as 'eight-wheeled rigids', constructed on Cleminson's Patent with side play for the axle boxes when taking curves. However normal bogie stock became the standard by the close of that decade, and in 1902 the Ashbury Carriage Co. supplied several trains of first class bogie stock, some of which survived until well into the 1950s. The final bogie stock was supplied by Cravens Ltd of Manchester in 1921, and was again used on the main line trains to Penarth. Many photographs show both sets of modern bogie stock in one train, the Craven stock usually for Merthyr, the low-roofed Ashbury stock for the Aberdare line.

Leaving the main line stock we return to the advent of the steam rail car era. Always known as steam motor cars by the TVR, car No. 1 was, as already recorded, initially worked on the Cardiff to Penarth and Sully service and, being such a success, cars Nos. 2 to 7 were added in 1904. These were also widely used on the Penarth service as they had composite bodies, whereas cars Nos. 8 to 13 were third class only, and did not normally work on the Penarth section, which had a much higher percentage of first class passengers than other sections of the TVR.

The cars proved so popular that a couple of lightweight non-driving trailer cars, Nos. 351 and 352 were supplied by the Bristol Wagon and Carriage Co. in 1905 to cater for the traffic developed. These proved the cars' downfall, particularly on the 1 in 40 incline up to Penarth, the cars not being designed or really capable of taking the trailer up such a severe bank, especially with a Motor Platform (Dingle Road) actually on the incline.

Hence a couple of years later Mr Tom Hurry Riches designed his somewhat 'Heath Robinson' type of overhead auto-gear, with masses of rods, wires and pulleys on top of the engine and trailer cars. He also designed the trailer cars, which were the largest passenger vehicles ever used on the TVR being 67 ft 8 in. in length. In the 1907 design the engine – one of the 'I' class 4–4–0Ts of 1884 – had a trailer car in front and behind the engine which, although successful, meant that throughout the day the driver was in the front of one of the trailer cars, controlling the train, whilst the fireman was similarly on his own on the engine.

TVR 'V' Class 0–6–0ST No. 99 shunting at Penarth Dock on 24th July, 1922. The 'V' class comprised six locomotives, built in 1899. *Courtesy Great Western Trust*

TVR 'I' Class 4–4–0T sandwiched between two 67 ft 8 ins. auto trailers. *The National Museum of Wales*

To avoid this arrangement, in 1910 Mr Riches decided to go in for a larger auto-train, two cars in front and two behind the engine which permitted one pair to be detached during off-peak periods, and allowed the driver to return to the engine when it was leading the train. The 4–4–0Ts were not considered powerful enough to work with four cars, so some of the older 'M1' class 0–6–2Ts, displaced from heavy main line work by the numerous more modern 0–6–2Ts, were auto-fitted. The 4–4–0Ts retained their auto fitting, and were still used on auto work when only a two car set was diagrammed. Mr Riches converted several 0–6–2Ts, far more than necessary to carry out the work, to ensure the auto-trains were never short of engine power, as the engines could be used on normal duties when not required for auto work.

Whilst there were now ample engines for auto work there was a shortage of cars, so in 1910 four old Thirds Nos. 301–304, were altered to work with the steam cars, one end compartment being converted into a driving compartment. This was a makeshift arrangement to prolong the life of some of the steam motors on the quieter branches, where turn-round time was not as vital as on the heavily used Penarth line. However that did not help the auto-train car shortage and 'Compo' Nos. 331 and 332 were also converted to trailer cars, whilst in 1912 two more of the large purpose built cars were acquired from the Gloucester C&W Co. There were then eight auto-trailers: the six purpose built cars, Nos. 78 to 80 and 353 to 355, together with Nos. 331/2, four 2 car sets only, and some eight or nine locos auto-fitted.

In 1914–6 the coach bodies were removed from eight of the steam motors, lengthened, and a bogie added where the body was formerly supported by the extended motor engine frame. The first pair were completed in August 1914 comprising cars Nos. 3 and 10, and were immediately put to work on the Penarth branch, particularly the lighter load section between Penarth and Cadoxton. Car No. 3 had a driving compartment whilst No. 10 was the intermediate trailer next to the locomotive. The main auto-train between Cardiff and Penarth comprised Driving 'Compo' Trailer No. 78 and intermediate Third Trailer No. 355, to which were added cars 3 and 10 when peak traffic was expected. It was in 1916 when the 4–4–2T of the 'C' class, Nos. 170–175, were auto-fitted, and they took over the four-car workings from the 0–6–2Ts. Thus by 1916 there were the equivalent of eight 2 car auto-sets, some used for part of the day at least as 4 car sets, and at least 15 engines-auto fitted: the six 4–4–2Ts Nos. 170–175, three 4–4–0Ts Nos. 285–287, and 0–6–2Ts Nos. 5, 14, 179, 180, 181 and 164 (later 364).

The remaining steam car coach bodies were removed in 1920, and altered similarly to the auto-trailers except that they were not auto-fitted but were formed with cars Nos. 8 and 12, from which the auto fittings were removed, into two corridor trains, the only ones on the TVR. The first of these trains comprising six cars was completed in 1921, the second, which entered service just at the time of the amalgamation in 1922 comprised four cars Nos. 6, 14, 15 and 16 and was immediately put in service on the Penarth branch. Its duties from Penarth began at 8.42 am with two businessmen's trains to Cardiff Clarence Road, after which it was laid aside until lunchtime. It then covered an afternoon and evening service to Cardiff, with one trip to Sully in the evening, finishing up at Penarth at 9.35 pm.

The Penarth auto-train worked throughout the day. It left Penarth Dock shed at 7.40 am and worked continuously between Cadoxton–Penarth–Cardiff until 11.15 pm; on Saturdays it worked on until 11.50 pm. One of the Coke Ovens (Pontypridd) auto-train rosters also took in workings on the same section between 7.00 am and 11.00 am. Another train that worked full time on the Penarth service was a 10 coach train of ex-Metropolitan District stock (which was one of four such trains purchased second-hand in 1906). This was based at Cathays but left Cardiff Queen St station for Penarth at 6.45 am and remained on the Penarth–Cardiff service until 6.20 pm.

Certainly there was a hectic passenger service on the Penarth branch when

Ex-TVR 'V' Class 0–6–0ST No. 791 (TVR No. 291) at Penarth Dock shed on 1st May, 1927, on a visit referred to in *Chapter 3*. *H.C. Casserley*

Ex-TVR 'K' Class 0–6–0 No. 920 (TVR No. 337) at Penarth Dock shed on 1st May, 1927. *H.C. Casserley*

the GWR took control in 1922, with some 40 trains in each direction between one of the Cardiff stations and Penarth. The 12.55 pm train, ex-Cardiff Clarence Road, was designated 'For Season Ticket Holders only'. In comparison there were only six trains each way on Sundays, with no service at all on the Penarth–Cadoxton section.

Since 1906 the 'Ports to Ports' express had worked between Barry and Newcastle, with GWR and Great Central stock on alternate week days. From the Summer Timetable of 1922 this train was re-routed via Penarth and, for the first time, GWR 4–4–0s of the 'Bulldog' and 'Flower' classes, together with 2–6–0s of the '43XX' class, could be seen at Penarth Town station where the train stopped at 9.20 am (up) and 7.00 pm (down). This only lasted for a couple of years or so, when the train was extended to Swansea and the Penarth diversion omitted. However it still passed over the former PHDR section between Penarth Curve South Jn and Cogan Jn which saw the greatest changes in motive power following the amalgamation. This

CARDIFF, PENARTH, & CADOXTON (TAFF VALE RAILWAY).

		M	M		M	M		M				Week Days.				M		M			M		M			M	
	am	a.m.	a.m.	a.m.	a.m.	a.m.	a m	a m	a.m.	a.m.	am	a.m.	a.m.	a.m.	a.m.	a.m.	a.m.	p.m.	p.m.	p.m.	p.m.	p.m.	pm	p.m.	p.m.	p.m.	p.m.
Car-diff Taff Vale dep	5 50	6 10	6 55	7 38	7 55	...	...	9 0	9 8	M	...	9 45	M	10 30	M	11 35	11 55	...	...	1 4	...	1 57	...	2 30	...	...	3 45
Car-diff G. W. R. ,,	5 55	6 15	6 59	7 44	8 0	.	.	9 5	9 15	.	.	9 50	.	10 36	.	11 40	12 1	.	.	1 9	.	2 3	.	2 34	.	.	3 50
Clarence Rd. dep	...	...	...	...	...	8 35	8 58	...	...	9 25	9 39	...	10 5	...	11 5	...	...	...	12 55	...	...	...	2 15	...	2 35	3 15	...
Cardiff Riv'side ,,	.	.	.	.	.	8 40	.	.	.	9 30	9 43	.	10 10	.	11 10	.	.	12 15	1 0	.	1 30	.	2 20	.	2 39	3 20	.
Grangetown dep	5 59	6 19	7 2	7 48	8 4	8 44	...	9 9	9 19	9 34	9 47	9 54	10 14	10 40	11 14	11 44	12 5	12 19	...	1 13	1 34	2 7	2 24	2 38	2 44	3 24	3 54
Penarth Dock ,,	6 5	6 24	7 6	7 54	8 8	8 48	.	9 13	9 25	9 38	9 53	10 0	10 18	10 46	11 18	11 48	12 11	12 23	1 7	1 18	1 38	2 13	2 28	2 44	2 52	3 28	4 0
Penarth ... ,,	6 11	6 28	7 11	7 58	8 15	8 55	9 10	9 16	9 29	9 49	9 57	10 4	10 25	10 50	11 23	11 53	12 15	12 30	1 11	1 28	1 43	2 17	2 35	2 53	2 57	3 33	4 9
Lower Penarth ,,	6 16	—	—	—	8 19	8 59	—	—	—	9 53	—	—	10 29	—	—	—	—	12 34	—	1 33	—	—	2 39	2 56	—	—	4 12
Lavernock ... ,,	6 20	...	...	...	8 23	9 3	...	...	...	9 57	...	...	10 33	...	...	...	...	12 38	...	1 37	...	...	—	3 0	...	...	4 16
Sully . ,,	6 25	.	.	.	8 27	9 7	.	.	.	10 1	.	.	10 37	.	.	.	.	12 42	.	1 42	.	.	—	3 5	.	.	4 21
Cadoxton arr	6 29	...	...	...	8 31	9 11	...	...	...	10 5	...	...	...	...	...	...	...	12 46	...	1 46	...	...	...	3 9	...	...	4 25

	M	M			M			M			Week Days.										Sundays.					
	p.m.	p.m.	p.m.	p.m.	p.m.	p.m.	p.m.	p.m.	p.m.	p.m.	p.m.	p.m.	p.m.	p.m.	p.m.	p.m.	p.m.	a.m.	a.m.	p.m.	p.m.	p.m.	p.m.	p.m.	p.m.	p.m.
Car-diff Taff Vale dep	...	...	4 25	5S10	...	5 30	6S5	6 18	6 40	7 5	7 35	8 21	8 45	9 30	10 18	10 45	11 0	9 30	9 40	1 5	2 50	4 30	5 50	7 0	8 10	9 55
Car-diff G.W.R. ,,	.	.	4 32	5S13	.	5 36	6S8	6 22	6 45	7 11	7 40	8 26	8 50	9 35	10 30	10 49	11 6	9 36	9 46	1 11	2 56	4 36	5 55	7 4	8 16	9 59
Clarence Rd. dep	4 7	4 35	...	5G10	5 27	...	6G5	...	...	...	...	...	...	...	...	...	...	...	...	...	...	...	...	...	...	...
Cardiff Riv'side ,,	4 12	4 41	.	5G14	5 32	.	6G10	.	.	.	.	.	.	.	.	.	.	.	.	.	.	.	.	.	.	.
Grangetown dep	4 16	4 45	4 38	...	5 36	5 40	6 15	6 26	6 49	7 15	7 44	8 30	8 54	9 39	10 34	10 52	11 10	9 40	9 50	1 15	3 0	4 40	5 58	7 8	8 20	10 4
Penarth Dock ,,	4 20	4 50	4 41	5 23	5 41	5 46	6 21	6 30	6 53	7 21	7 48	8 35	9 0	9 45	10 40	10 56	11 16	9 46	9 56	1 21	3 6	4 46	6 12	7 14	8 26	10 9
Penarth ... ,,	4 25	4 58	4 45	5 27	5 45	6 0	6 25	6 35	6 57	7 25	7 52	8 39	9 10	9 49	10 44	11 1	11 20	9 50	10 10	1 25	3 11	4 50	6 33	7 18	8 30	10 13
Lower Penarth ,,	—	5 2	—	—	—	6 4	—	—	—	7 38	}	—	9 14	}	—	—	—	—	10 13	—	3 14	—	6 36	—	—	—
Lavernock ... ,,	...	5 6	...	...	...	6 8	...	...	...	7 42	M	...	9 18	M	...	...	...	...	10 17	...	3 18	...	6 40	.	...	...
Sully . ,,	.	5 10	.	.	.	6 13	.	.	.	7 47	}	.	9 22	}	.	.		.	10 22	.	3 23	.	6 45	...	.	.
Cadoxton arr	...	5 14	...	...	...	6 17	...	...	...	7 51		...	9 26		...	...	...	...	10 26	...	3 27	...	6 49	.	...	.

		M						M				M	Week Days.					M	M			M		M		M	
	a.m.	a.m.	am	a.m.	a.m.	a.m.	a.m.	a.m.	a.m.	a.m.	a.m.	a.m.	a.m.	a.m.	a.m.	p.m.	p.m.	p.m.	pm	p.m.	p.m.	pm	p.m.	pm	p.m.	p.m.	p.m.
Cadoxton....dep	...	...	6 55	...	...	...	...	8 48	...	9 22	...	10 15	M	...	...	...	...	12 55	...	...	2 0	...	...	3 20	...	...	...
Sully . . ,,	.	.	7 0	.	.	.	.	8 52	.	9 26	.	10 19	10 46	.	M	.	.	12 59	.	.	2 4	.	.	3 24	.	.	.
Lavernock . . ,,	...	...	7 5	...	...	...	...	8 56	...	9 30	...	10 23	10 50	...	...	...	...	1 3	...	...	2 9	...	...	3 28	...	...	...
Lower Penarth ,,	.	.	7 9	.	.	.	.	8 58	.	9 34	.	10 27	10 54	.	.	.	.	1 7	.	.	2 13	2 50	.	3 32	.	.	.
Penarth ... ,,	5 25	6 35	7 20	7 40	8 0	8 30	8 40	9 4	9 18	9 45	10 10	10 40	11 0	11 30	11 45	12 15	12 35	1 14	1 50	2 10	2 20	2 55	3 10	3 38	3 43	4 10	4 35
Penarth Dock ,,	5 29	6 39	7 24	7 44	8 4	8 34	8 44	9 8	9 22	9 49	10 14	10 45	11 4	11 34	11 49	12 19	12 39	1 18	1 54	2 14	2 24	2 59	3 14	3 42	3 47	4 14	4 39
Grangetown ,,	5 34	6 44	7 29	...	8 8	8 39	...	9 13	...	9 53	10 19	10 50	11 9	11 39	11 53	12 24	12 44	1 22	1 58	2 20	2 29	3 3	3 19	3 46	3 52	4 19	4 44
Cardiff Riv's'de dep	.	.	.	.	8 11	.	8 51	9 17	9 30	9 57	.	10 58	...	.	11 56	12 30	.	1 25	2 5	2 27	.	3 7	.	3 50	.	4 24	4G50
Clarence Road arr	...	...	...	...	8 14	...	8 54	9 20	9 33	10 0	...	11 2	.	...	—	12 33	...	—	2 8	2 30	...	3 10	...	3 53	...	4 27	4G53
Car-diff G.W.R. arr	5 37	6 47	7 32	7 50	.	8 42	.	.	.	.	10 22	...	11 12	11 42	...	.	12 47	.	.	.	2 32	.	3 22	.	3 58	...	4S50
Car-diff Taff Vale ,,	5 41	6 52	7 42	8 0	...	8 50	...	...	...	...	10 30	.	11 17	11 50	.	...	12 55	...	...	...	2 40	...	3 29	...	4 1	.	4S55

	M			M		M			Week Days.				M		M					Sundays.						
	p.m.	p.m.	p.m.	p.m.	p.m.	p.m.	p.m.	p.m.	p.m.	p.m.	p.m.	p.m.	p.m.	p.m.	p.m.	a.m.	a.m.	a.m.	p.m.	p.m.	p.m.	p.m.		p.m.		p.m.
Cadoxton dep	...	4 52	...	5 32	...	...	6 40	}	...	...	8 40	...	9 40	...	...	...	...	10 50	...	4 0	...	7 35	...	...	...	...
Sully . . ,,	.	4 56	.	5 36	.	.	6 44	M	.	.	8 44	.	9 44	.	.	.	.	10 54	.	4 4	.	7 39	.	.	.	.
Lavernock ,,	...	5 1	...	5 40	...	...	6 48	M	...	...	8 48	...	9 48	...	...	...	...	10 59	...	4 9	...	7 44	...	...	...	...
Lower Penarth ,,	.	5 5	.	5 44	.	.	6 52	}	.	.	8 52	.	9 52	.	.	.	.	11 3	.	4 13	.	7 48	.	.	.	.
Penarth ... ,,	4 55	5 10	5 31	5 50	6 32	6 44	7 0	7 30	7 45	8 25	9 15	9 45	10 0	10 30	11 8	8 15	10 20	11 7	2 18	4 20	5 55	7 52	...	9 5	...	9 16
Penarth Dock ,,	4 59	5 14	5 35	5 54	6 36	6 48	7 4	7 34	7 49	8 29	9 19	9 49	10 6	10 34	11 12	8 19	10 24	11 11	2 22	4 24	5 59	7 56	.	9 9	.	[illegible]
Grangetown ,,	5 3	5 19	5 40	5 58	6 41	6 52	7 9	7 39	7 54	8 34	9 24	9 54	10 10	10 39	11 16	8 25	10 30	11 17	2 28	4 30	6 5	8 2	...	9 15	...	9 20
Cardiff Riv's'de dep	5 7	.	5G46	.	.	...	.	.	.	.	.	.	.	.	...	.	.	.	.	.	.	.	.	.	...	.
Clarence Road arr	5 10	...	5G49	...	...	.	...	...	...	...	...	..	...	...	.	...	...	...	...	...	...	...	...	...	.	...
Car-diff G.W.R. arr	...	5 22	5S46	6 1	6 44	6 55	7 12	7 42	7 57	8 37	9 27	9 57	10 13	10 42	11 19	8 28	10 33	11 20	2 31	4 33	6 8	8 5	.	9 18	.	[illegible]
Car-diff Taff Vale ,,	.	5 30	5S49	6 5	6 31	6 59	7 19	7 49	8 1	8 43	9 33	10 6	10 17	10 50	11 23	8 34	10 38	11 25	2 36	4 41	6 13	8 12	...	9 23	...	[illegible]

G—Saturdays excepted. M—Rail Motor Car. S—Saturdays only.

The TVR Cardiff–Penarth–Cadoxton train service as shown in the GWR public timetable for October 1905. Although the 'Rail Motor Cars' are shown, the 'Motor Platforms' open at that time, i.e. Llandough, Dingle Road and Alberta Place, are omitted.

Two more locomotives at Penarth Dock shed on 1st May, 1927; nearer the camera is ex-Barry Railway 'A' Class 0–6–0T Nos. 699 (Barry Railway No. 1), while beyond is ex-TVR 'N' Class 0–6–2T No. 500 (TVR No. 187), still fitted with the TVR system of auto-train control apparatus. *H.C. Casserley*

A down four-car auto-train approaching Lower Penarth in GWR days, with two GWR clerestory-roofed cars leading. The locomotive, between the two sets of two cars, appears to be an outside-framed 0–6–0PT. *H.T. Hobbs (R.C. Riley Collection)*

was because of the massive volume of excursion traffic to Barry Island which passed over that section of line, hauled by almost every class of GWR engine, apart from 'Kings' and '47XX' class 2–8–0s, both of which classes were barred in South Wales. The 'Kings' did work to Cardiff from 1957 onwards, but never to Barry except Nos. 6023 and 6024 which were towed to Woodham's yard late in 1962 (both these engines were later bought for preservation). 'Castle' and 'Hall' class 4–6–0s frequently worked through to Barry Island, whilst in BR days even the occasional 'Britannia' class 4–6–2 worked through from Paddington.

GWR engines had occasionally been seen over the section *en route* to Barry even before the grouping. Certain excursions to Barry Island were worked by GW engines; early in 1921 2–6–2Ts Nos. 3119, 3129 and 3140 were on loan to the Barry Railway and 2–8–0T No. 4254 was tried out on a 50 wagon coal train between Bridgend and Barry.

At Grouping there was an allocation of 21 engines at Penarth Dock shed. There were eight of the modern 'A' class passenger tanks, together with two auto-fitted engines, whilst four of the six heavy duty shunting engines of the 'V' class were also there. The full list, giving the allocated GW engine numbers in brackets was:

0–6–2T	'A' class	11(343) 12(344) 125(360) 159(381) 400(386) 401(387) 402(388) 404(390)
0–6–2T	'O4' class	17(283) 94(296) 119(324)
0–6–2T	'M1' class	15(445) 179(491)* 365(586)
4–4–2T	'C' class	172(1303)*
0–6–0ST	'V' class	99(786) 100(787) 280(789) 290(790)
0–6–0	'K' class	217(922) 354(974)

*auto-fitted

The principal change over the next five years was that the Taff Vale 0–6–2Ts on mineral work were replaced by former Barry Railway 0–6–2Ts. In July 1926 double frame Standard Goods No. 1202 was shedded at Penarth (until October), whilst Dean Goods No. 2446 worked from the shed from March 1927 until April 1928 and was the last tender engine allocated there. The last Taff Vale 0–6–0 tender engine, No. 920, was withdrawn from Penarth Shed in December 1927.

A visit paid to the shed on 1st May, 1927 found 24 engines there although one, at least, was a 'visitor', not in the Penarth allocation. The list was:

0–6–2T	TVR	'A'	class	377 386 394 401 408
	"	'N'	class	500* 502
0–6–0ST	TVR	'V'	class	786 788 789 790 791
0–6–0	"	'K'	class	920
0–6–2T	BARRY	'B/B1'	class	203 223 227 228 232 255
0–6–0T	"	'A'	class	699 703
0–6–0PT	GWR			120
2–6–2T	"			3913
0–6–0	"			2446

*TVR auto-fitted

An up two-coach auto-train leaving Lower Penarth in 1936, formed of a GWR 0–6–0PT propelling two ex-TVR auto-trailers. *H.T. Hobbs (R.C. Riley Collection)*

A down train entering Dingle Road in early GWR days, formed of an ex-TVR 'A' class 0–6–2T, rebuilt with GWR boiler and bunker, hauling GWR clerestory roofed coaches. *H.T. Hobbs (R.C. Riley Collection)*

CARDIFF, PENARTH, LAVERNOCK, and CADOXTON

Down — mrn — Week Days — aft

Miles	HOUR	5	M 6	6	7	7	7	X 7 M	8	8	9	M 9	10	10	M 10	11	11	11	M 11	M 12	12	12	L 1	1	M 1	1	1	L 2	2	2	2	2	M 3	3	S 3	3	4	M 4	4
—	Cardiff (Queen St.)..dep.	.	.	37	.	20	37	.	5	35	3	43	.	18	.	16	.	43	57	.	.	.	.	0	.	.	57	16	.	.	35	44	.	21	.	47	5	25	.
1	" (General)	.	.	42	.	26	42	.	8	43	8	48	.	27	.	19	.	55	**0**	.	.	.	.	8	.	.	**4**	19	.	.	45	47	.	28	.	52	8	30	.
—	Cardiff { Clar. Rd.dp.	.	.	.	16	.	.	.	.	.	.	.	15	.	.	.	15	.	.	.	20	52	.	.	.	.	.	.	E20	E37	.	.	E14	.	.	.	.	.	E30
—	Cardiff { Riverside A	45	.	.	21	.	.	.	.	.	.	.	19	.	.	.	24	.	.	.	25	57	.	.	.	33	.	.	25	41	.	.	18	.	.	.	.	.	37
2	Grangetown	49	.	47	25	31	47	.	.	48	13	53	.	32	.	.	28	**0**	.	.	29	**1**	.	13	.	37	9	.	29	45	50	.	22	33	.	57	.	35	41
3½	Penarth Dock B ¶	53	21	51	29	35	.	.	.	52	17	57	26	36	.	.	.	.	.	.	33	.	.	.	.	41	.	.	.	49	54	.	.	.	.	**1**	.	.	45
4½	Penarth ¶ { arr.	57	25	55	33	39	54	.	.	56	21	**3**	30	40	.	.	37	7	.	.	39	10	.	22	.	47	16	.	36	53	58	.	31	40	.	5	.	44	49
	Penarth ¶ { dep.	.	26	**0**	34	.	.	56	.	**0**	.	6	.	.	50	.	38	.	.	10	.	11	.	.	24	.	18	.	38	.	**5**	.	.	47	57	6	.	.	.
6½	Lavernock ¶	.	32	6	40	.	.	**4**	.	8	.	14	.	.	58	.	44	.	.	18	.	.	.	.	32	.	24	.	44	.	11	.	.	53	**3**	12	.	.	.
8½	Sully	.	37	12	46	.	.	10	.	14	.	20	.	.	**4**	.	50	.	.	24	.	23	24	.	38	.	30	.	50	.	17	.	.	**0**	9	.	.	.	.
9½	Cadoxton 97.......arr.	.	.	16	.	.	.	14	.	18	.	.	.	.	8	.	.	.	.	28	.	.	28	.	42	.	.	.	.	.	21	.	.	3	.	.	.	.	.

aft — Week Days—*Continued* — mrn — Sundays — aft

HOUR	M 4	4	5	5	5	M 6	5	6	6	6	M 7	7	Y 7 K	7	M 8	8	8	M 9	9	10	M 10	11	X 9	9	X 10	10	11	X 11	X 12	1	1	2	X 3	4	X 4	5	6	6	8	8	9	K 10
Cardiff (Queen St.) .dep.	.	54	.	.	35	.	.	4	27	45	.	18	24	48	.	35	55	.	38	16	50	.	30	40	7	47	12	32	28	10	55	25	20	31	45	10	10	40	0	40	50	50
" (General)	.	59	.	.	43	.	.	7	33	50	.	26	33	53	.	44	**5**	.	43	27	55	.	35	45	12	52	18	37	33	15	**0**	30	25	34	52	15	15	45	5	45	55	55
Cardiff { Clar. Rd.dp.	.	.	E5	E25	.	E	53	20	E	.	.	.	.	.	.	.	.	.	.	.	.	.	.	.	.	.	.	.	.	.	.	.	.	.	.	.	.	.	.	.	.	.
Cardiff { Riverside A	.	.	9	30	.	.	58	24	.	.	.	.	.	.	.	.	.	.	.	.	.	15	.	.	.	.	.	.	.	.	.	.	.	.	.	.	.	.	.	.	.	.
Grangetown	.	**4**	13	Ss	48	.	.	28	38	55	.	31	.	58	.	49	10	.	48	32	**0**	19	40	50	17	57	23	42	38	20	5	35	30	.	57	20	20	50	10	50	**0**	**0**
Penarth Dock B ¶	.	.	17	.	.	.	**5**	.	.	.	.	35	**2**	.	.	.	.	.	.	36	.	.	.	.	.	.	.	.	.	.	9	.	.	.	.	.	.	.	.	.	.	.
Penarth ¶ { arr.	.	13	23	42	57	.	11	37	45	**4**	.	40	45	8	.	58	19	.	57	42	7	26	47	57	24	**4**	30	49	45	27	13	42	37	.	**4**	27	27	57	17	57	7	7
Penarth ¶ { dep.	50	.	.	43	.	2	.	41	.	.	5	.	47	.	17	.	.	20	.	.	H8	.	50	.	26	.	35	50	46	29	14	44	38	.	6	.	28	**0**	19	59	.	8
Lavernock ¶	58	.	.	51	.	10	.	47	.	.	13	.	.	.	25	.	.	28	.	.	16	H	56	.	32	.	41	56	52	35	20	50	44	.	12	.	34	6	25	**5**	.	.
Sully	**4**	.	.	57	.	16	.	53	.	.	19	.	.	.	31	.	.	34	.	.	22	H	**2**	.	38	.	47	**2**	58	41	25	56	50	.	18	.	40	12	31	11	.	.
Cadoxton 97 ......arr.	8	.	.	.	.	20	.	.	.	.	23	.	**2**	.	35	.	.	38	.	.	.	.	6	.	42	.	51	5	**2**	.	.	**0**	54	.	22	.	.	16	.	16	.	22

Up — mrn — Week Days — aft

HOUR	5	6	6	M 6	7	7	8	8	8	8	X 8 M	M 9	9	9	10	M 10	10	11	Y 11 R	11	M 11	11	M 12	12	12	12	1	S 2	L 1	2	M 2	2	3	M 2	2	3	M 3	3	4	4	5
Cadoxton..........dep.	.	.	.	.	.	25	.	.	.	.	41	.	.	35	.	.	.	.	8	.	28	.	.	.	.	50	.	.	50	.	20	.	.	.	.	.	.	40	.	.	.
Sully ¶	.	.	.	47	.	29	.	.	20	.	45	.	.	39	.	30	.	.	.	.	32	.	.	8	.	54	.	.	55	2	24	.	.	.	55	25	.	44	.	S25	.
Lavernock	.	.	.	54	.	36	.	.	27	.	52	.	.	46	.	37	.	.	.	.	39	.	.	15	.	**1**	.	.	.	8	31	.	.	.	**2**	32	.	51	18	S32	.
Penarth ¶ { arr.	.	.	.	**1**	.	45	.	.	35	.	**0**	.	.	55	.	45	.	.	23	.	48	.	.	22	.	10	.	.	.	16	40	.	.	.	9	39	.	58	24	S39	.
Penarth ¶ { dep.	15	25	50	2	31	46	.	13	37	45	2	13	30	56	30	.	48	15	25	35	.	50	.	25	37	13	52	.	.	17	.	41	.	56	32	42	54	**5**	27	40	.
Penarth Dock B	18	28	53	6	35	50	.	17	42	.	.	.	33	.	34	.	51	19	.	.	.	54	.	29	.	17	56	.	.	.	.	45	.	**0**	35	46	58	.	31	43	.
Grangetown	22	32	57	10	39	54	.	21	46	.	.	20	.	.	38	.	55	23	.	41	.	58	.	33	.	21	**0**	.	.	S24	.	49	.	4	39	50	**2**	.	35	47	.
Cardiff { Riverside A	26	36	.	14	.	.	.	.	50	.	14	.	40	**6**	.	.	59	.	.	.	.	**1**	.	37	.	25	4	.	.	27	.	.	.	8	.	54	.	.	.	51	.
Cardiff { Clar. Rd arr.	.	40	.	.	.	.	.	.	54	.	17	.	44	10	.	.	**3**	.	.	.	.	8	.	47	.	.	E10	.	.	E31	.	.	.	E12	E	59	.	.	.	E58	.
Cardiff (Gen.) 64, 80..	.	.	**9**	.	44	**0**	13	27	.	56	.	27	.	.	43	.	.	28	41	46	.	.	5	.	48	.	.	23	.	.	.	58	10	.	45	.	9	16	40	.	3
" (Qn St.) 82,84,90 arr.	.	.	13	.	56	4	16	30	.	**0**	.	30	.	.	50	.	.	33	44	53	.	.	8	.	56	.	.	26	.	.	.	**1**	13	.	53	.	12	23	46	.	6

aft — Week Days—*Continued* — mrn — Sundays — aft

HOUR	5	4	5	M 5	5	6	M 6	6	7	M 7	8	M 8	9	L 9	9	M 10	10	11	H 11 M	6	7	10	11	X 11	12	1	X 1	2	3	4	X 4	5	6	7	R 7	8	9	10	R 9	10
Cadoxton..........dep	.	53	.	28	.	.	35	.	.	45	.	44	.	.	.	0	.	.	.	.	.	.	.	6	8	.	56	.	45	.	21	.	.	25	56	.	42	.	56	.
Sully ¶	.	57	.	32	.	10	39	.	10	49	.	48	.	.	.	4	.	.	30	.	.	.	.	10	12	50	**0**	35	49	.	25	.	48	29	**0**	40	46	.	**0**	.
Lavernock	.	**4**	.	39	.	17	46	.	17	56	.	55	.	.	.	11	.	.	.	.	.	.	.	17	19	57	7	42	56	.	32	.	55	36	7	47	53	.	7	.
Penarth ¶ { arr.	.	11	.	48	.	23	55	.	24	**5**	.	**4**	.	.	.	18	.	.	42	.	.	.	.	24	23	**3**	14	48	**3**	.	38	.	**1**	43	13	53	59	.	13	.
Penarth ¶ { dep.	0	13	28	.	56	27	.	56	35	6	30	.	6	.	45	20	38	35	.	.	45	12	10	25	28	4	15	50	9	.	40	45	2	44	16	55	.	2	.	16
Penarth Dock B	3	17	31	.	**0**	31	.	.	39	9	33	.	9	.	48	23	41	.	.	.	.	.	.	.	.	.	.	.	12	.	.	.	.	.	.	.	.	.	.	.
Grangetown	7	21	35	.	4	35	.	**3**	43	13	37	.	13	.	52	27	45	41	.	.	51	18	16	31	34	10	22	56	16	.	46	51	8	50	22	**1**	.	8	.	22
Cardiff { Riverside A	11	.	39	.	9	.	.	.	.	.	.	.	.	.	.	.	.	45	.	.	.	.	.	.	.	.	.	.	.	.	.	.	.	.	.	.	.	.	.	.
Cardiff { Clar. Rd arr.	E18	.	E44	.	E13	.	.	.	.	.	.	.	.	.	.	.	.	.	.	.	.	.	.	.	.	.	.	.	.	.	.	.	.	.	.	.	.	.	.	.
Cardiff (Gen.) 64, 80..	.	N26	.	.	.	39	.	8	48	18	42	.	18	57	58	32	50	.	.	35	56	23	21	36	39	15	27	**1**	20	47	51	56	13	55	27	6	.	13	.	27
" (Qn St.) 82,84,90 arr.	.	37	.	.	.	46	.	18	56	23	48	.	24	**1**	**4**	37	**0**	.	.	38	**4**	28	26	48	44	20	32	6	29	50	56	**1**	18	**0**	32	12	.	18	.	32

A Adjoins G. W. Main Line Sta **B** Adjoins Cogan Sta E or Ɛ Except Sats H or H Weds Thurs and Sats
K To Barry, page 86 L Weds. and Sats. M One class only
N Dep 5 34 aft R From Barry, page 86 S or S Sats only
Ss Stops Sats only X To and from Barry Island, page 86
Y On 16th, 23rd, and 30th inst. Thro' Train to and from Llandrindod Wells (one class only), page 86, 87, 150, 492, & 493.

¶ **"Halts"** at Dingle Road, between Penarth Dock and Penarth at Alberta Place and at Lower Penarth, between Penarth and Lavernock and at Swanbridge, between Lavernock and Sully

OTHER TRAINS between Cardiff and Cadoxton, see page 86

Where the MINUTES under the Hours change to a LOWER figure and DARKER type it indicates the NEXT HOUR

Bradshaw's timetable for July 1938.

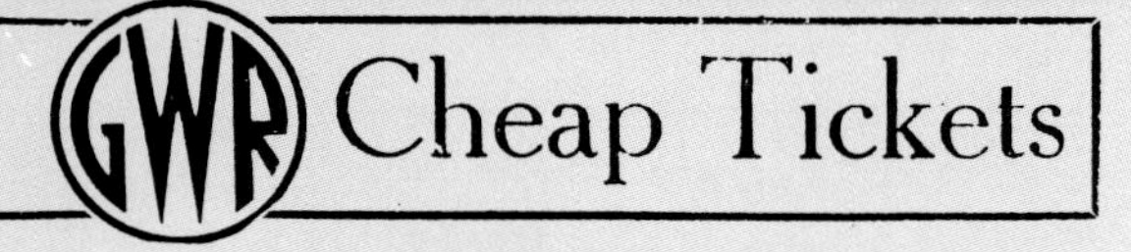

WILL BE ISSUED TO

PENARTH

ON

Tuesdays, Wednesdays and Thursdays,
AUGUST 13th to 29th
(both dates inclusive)

Stations From	Trains leaving		Return Fares, Third Class.	Stations From	Trains leaving at		Return Fares, Third Class.
	a.m.	a.m.	s. d.		a.m.	a.m.	s. d.
Treherbert	9 0	10 [illegible]	[illegible]	Troedyrhiw	8 32	10 23	4 4
Treorchy	9 4	10 [illegible]	[illegible]	Merthyr Vale	8 38	10 33	4 0
Ystrad (Rhondda)	9 8	10 27	[illegible]	Quakers Yd. (L.L.)	8 45	10 44	3 8
Llwynypia	9 13	10 [illegible]	[illegible]	Aberdare (L.L.) B.	8 25	10 25	4 8
Tonypandy	9 17	10 [illegible]	[illegible]	Aberaman	8 30	10 28	4 7
Dinas	9 19	10 [illegible]	[illegible]	M'tain Ash (Ox St.)	8 36	10 34	4 1
Maerdy } A.	9 0	10 [illegible]	[illegible]	Penrhiwceiber (L.L.)	8 40	10 39	3 11
Ferndale } A.	9 6	10 [illegible]	[illegible]	Abercynon	8 55	10 55	3 4
Tylorstown } A.	9 11	10 [illegible]	[illegible]	Pontypridd	9 39	11 8	2 9
Ynishir } A.	9 16	10 [illegible]	[illegible]	Treforest	9 42	11 13	2 7
Porth	9 25	10 [illegible]	[illegible]	Taffs Well	9 51	11 20	1 9
Trehafod	9 28	10 [illegible]	[illegible]	Radyr	9 55	11 24	1 5
Merthyr } B.	8 25	10 25	[illegible]	Llandaff	9 59	11 28	1 3
Pentrebach } B.	8 29	10 30	[illegible]				
						p.m.	
				Penarth Town arr.	10 27	12 7	

A—Change at Porth. B—Change at Pontypridd.

PASSENGERS RETURN FROM PENARTH at 7.0 p.m. and 8.30 p.m.

Children under Three Years of age, Free; Three and under Fourteen years, Half-Fare.

NOTICE AS TO CONDITIONS.

Tickets are available for Day of issue only, and are not Transferable—Break of journey not allowed.

These tickets are issued subject to the conditions of issue of ordinary passenger tickets where applicable, and also to the special conditions as set out in the Ticket, etc., Regulations, By-Laws and General Notices. Luggage allowances are as set out in these General Notices.

Any further information may be obtained from Mr. H. H. Swift, Divisional Superintendent, Cardiff (Queen Street) Telephone: Cardiff 8100, Extension 310; or from Mr. Gilbert Matthews, Superintendent of the Line, Paddington Station, W.2. (Telephone: Paddington 7000, Extn. "Enquiries," 8.0 a.m. to 10.0 p.m.).

Paddington, August, 1946.

JAMES MILNE,
General Manager.

Cheap Tickets to Penarth advertised by the GWR after World War II, in August 1946.
The National Museum of Wales, Harris Collection

ASSOCIATION FOOTBALL
ENGLISH LEAGUE DIV. 2
Cardiff City v Rotherham Utd.
AT NINIAN PARK, CARDIFF
KICK-OFF 7.15 p.m.

British Railways
WESTERN REGION

FRIDAY, 17 JANUARY, 1964

FOOTBALL EXCURSION
TO
NINIAN PARK HALT

FROM	DEPART	RETURN FARES SECOND CLASS
	p.m.	s. d.
RHYMNEY	5 25	5 3
PONTLOTTYN	5 30	5 0
TIRPHIL	5 38	4 9
BRITHDIR	5 43	4 6
BARGOED	5 50	4 0
PENGAM (Glam.)	5 55	3 9
HENGOED (L.L.)	6 0	3 6
YSTRAD MYNACH	6 3	3 3
LLANBRADACH	6 10	2 6
ABER JUNCTION HALT	6 17	2 3
CAERPHILLY	6 20	2 0
LLANISHEN	6 28	1 5
HEATH HALT (H.L.)	6 33	1 2
LLANDAFF	6A26	1 3
CARDIFF (Queen St.)	6 40	9
CARDIFF (Gen.)	6 45	9
NEWPORT	6B11	2 9
	p.m.	
NINIAN PARK HALT arr.	6 55	

Return from Ninian Park Halt 9.5 p.m. same day.

Notes: A Change at Cardiff (Queen St.) in each direction.
B Change at Cardiff (Gen.) in each direction.

Passengers may also return from Cardiff (Gen.) or (Queen St.) by any other train same day, affording a service through to destination.

Children under fourteen years of age, half-fare

Information and tickets can be obtained in advance from Stations or Agencies

Further details from Mr. R. C. Hilton, Divisional Manager, Room 161, Marland House, Central Square, Cardiff (Tel: Cardiff 21021, Ext. 2411)

Paddington Station, W2.
December, 1963.

G. F. FIENNES,
General Manager.

A Football excursion to Ninian Park from the Rhymney line, with connections from Llandaff and Newport, on 17th January, 1964, as shown on a Western Region handbill.

Of the above No. 500 was the last TVR type auto-fitted engine to work from Penarth shed; No. 3913 was a Treherbert engine, and had probably worked a train to Penarth and, being a Sunday, was on shed waiting its return working.

Despite the large number of '56XX' class 0–6–2Ts built to replace the older absorbed engines, none settled for any length of time at Penarth, until the Autumn of 1928. The first shedded there was No. 5625 in December 1925 but left the following month for Treherbert. It was almost a year before the next one came, No. 5627 in October 1926, and that lasted only a month also. A further 12 months elapsed before Nos. 5634 and 5663 were transferred to Penarth in December 1927 lasting only one, and two, months respectively before moving on elsewhere. Finally in September 1928, when the Taff 'A' class tanks were being sent to Barry shed to replace the old Barry passenger engines, Nos. 6621, 6622, 6641, 6642, 6650 and 6652 were all sent to Penarth, Nos. 6641 and 6642 being new from Swindon Works. The six GW 0–6–2Ts then remained as the top link engines at the shed until it closed early in 1929. The official closure date was 13th February, 1929, but the records indicate that the engines remained working from the shed until early April. Even after that it must have remained as a servicing point for several months, as the shed was not vacated by the Locomotive Dept until 22nd October, 1929.

On the occasion of a private visit to the shed on Easter Sunday 31st March, 1929, there were 21 engines present, nearly all being 0–6–2Ts:

TVR	0–6–2T	'M1'	class	506 567 573 577 (All GW auto-fitted)
"	0–6–0ST	'V'	class	789
BARRY	0–6–2T	'B/B1'	class	204 206 223 228 232 241 255
"	0–6–0T	'A'	class	699
"	0–6–0ST	'F'	class	722 726 747
GWR	0–6–2T			6621 6622 6642 6650 6652

No. 567 was a Cathays engine, and No. 577 was shedded at Coke Ovens, the others were all allocated to Penarth and were dispersed over the following week to Cardiff East Dock and other sheds in the Cardiff area.

Although Radyr shed can only be described as 'loosely connected' to the Penarth workings, it is interesting to note that its allocation in 1922, when the GWR took control, was 25 engines of which no less than 17 were 0–6–0 tender engines, and one other a departmental locomotive for shunting the permanent way depot at Radyr. The other seven engines were 0–6–2Ts. Under the GWR the tender engines were quickly withdrawn and replaced by 0–6–2Ts, there is no record that any of the GW 0–6–0s, either Standard or Dean Goods, was ever sent to Radyr as a replacement for a Taff tender engine. Radyr yard became even more important under the GWR, and the old Taff Vale engine shed near the station was closed on 29th March, 1931, when it was replaced by a modern four road shed sited between the permanent way yard and the large storage and sorting sidings.

Returning to the post-amalgamation passenger services on the Penarth lines, the use of auto-trains increased, with the Taff system of overhead rods and wires gradually giving way, from early 1926 onwards, to the GWR

The 9.13 am train to Cardiff (Clarence Road) about to leave Penarth Town on 30th April, 1958, propelled by ex-GWR 0–6–0PT No. 6438. The JB 'target' denotes a working based on Abercynon shed. Note, beyond station footbridge, GWR-type signals attached to Stanwell Road bridge, and compare with photograph on *page 34*.
R.O. Tuck

A Cardiff to Cadoxton train leaving Penarth Town on 17th February, 1958 formed of ex-GWR 2–6–2T No. 4122 and five non-corridor coaches. This photograph shows the location of the carriage sidings, goods yard and goods shed. *R.O. Tuck*

Ex-GWR 0–6–0PT No. 6438 standing at Grangetown station with a Cardiff–Penarth service on 2nd May, 1958. *M. Hale, courtesy Great Western Trust*

The 6.45 am Fishguard Harbour to Paddington train, diverted between Bridgend and Cardiff via the Vale of Glamorgan line and Barry, crossing the bridge over the river Ely between Cogan Junction and Grangetown on Sunday, 4th May, 1958, hauled by ex-GWR 'Castle' class 4–6–0 No. 5051 *Earl Bathurst*. The bridge being traversed by the train is that constructed in 1904 for the quadrupling of this section of line, referred to in *Chapter 1*. *R.O. Tuck*

BR-built (GWR design) 2–6–2T No. 4177 on the down platform line at Penarth Town in 1957. *H.T. Hobbs (R.C. Riley Collection)*

Ex-GWR 0–6–2T No. 5634 passing the site of the present day Danescourt station with a returning Football Special from Ninian Park to Merthyr Tydfil in the early 1960s. Passing on the down line is empty stock *en route* from Radyr to Ninian Park for another similar special train. *A.F. Smith, Peter Rowe (Printers), Cardiff*

'under the frame' control gear. By early 1927 most of the Taff auto-fitted engines had either been scrapped, or converted to the GWR system at Swindon. No record has been found of when the Taff system was last used but it was probably in the Spring of 1927. Eric Mountford's friend, Phil Reed, recorded that he travelled to Penarth Dock station in a two-car Taff set on his visit to the engine shed on 24th August, 1926. The engine on that occasion was 'N' class 0–6–2T No. 500, which certainly still retained its TVR control gear in 1927, and probably did so until it was withdrawn in 1928. However it seems unlikely that its auto gear was used after Spring 1927, as the conversion of Taff cars at Swindon to the GWR control system was spread out over the period 1924 to 1927; the surviving cars had certainly all been altered, before the last auto-fitted engines were withdrawn.

The Rhymney and Barry trailer cars were also fitted with the GWR system in the same period although the Barry cars only rarely used the Penarth Town section. However it was not uncommon to see a four-car set comprising two Taff cars one side of the engine and two Rhymney cars on the other. With many GWR auto-fitted 0–6–0PTs and 2–4–0Ts drafted on to the Taff section, it was frequently possible to see a GWR engine sandwiched between Taff and Rhymney sets. The Taff engines which had been fitted with GWR auto control gear, had all been withdrawn by 1934, by which time the purpose-built auto-engines of the '64XX' and '48XX' classes had begun to appear. The former were the favourites for the work in the old Taff Vale area until a regular interval passenger service was introduced in the Cardiff Valleys section in British Railways days, in September 1953. A number of the small wheeled 2–6–2Ts of the '4575' class were then auto-fitted and drafted into the area to replace the '64XX' workings, where rapid acceleration from the frequent stops was required. Even so the '64XXs' remained very much in evidence on local auto services around Cardiff and Penarth.

The main passenger service between the Rhymney Valley and Penarth did not fit into the regular interval pattern for several years; even so the motive power was changed, standard GWR 2–6–2Ts of the '41XX' series being shedded at Rhymney to replace the Taff 'A' class and GW '56XX' class 0–6–2Ts, on all but certain peak period workings. Those transferred to Rhymney were Nos. 4101, 4143, 4160–4163 and, for a few months, No. 5195. These worked regularly to Penarth, but the BR Standard class '3' 2–6–2Ts of the '82XXX' series which were drafted into Barry shed at the same time to work the service between the Taff Valleys and Barry Island, only visited Penarth on rare occasions. They could be regularly seen, however, on the old PHDR section between Cogan and Penarth Curve Junctions. Nevertheless there was still a wide variety of engines to be seen at Penarth in the mid-1950s, with the '41XX' class on the principal passenger services, but '56XX' and Taff 'A's on relief work, both '55XX' and '64XX' on auto workings, and pannier tanks or the '56XX' class on the local goods.

Over the years the carriage stock had, naturally, changed also. Although former Rhymney and Barry Railway carriages were to be seen at Penarth within a few years of Grouping, Taff bogie stock dominated the formation of the main passenger services until the late-1920s, and, on a gradually reducing scale, well into the 1930s. They were gradually replaced by GWR stan-

Ex-GWR 0–6–0 No. 2218 hauling a down Football Special to Ninian Park passing the site of the present day Fairwater station on 18th October, 1958. The third coach is one of the low-roofed vehicles built by the GWR for the Burry Port and Gwendraeth Valley line (Burry Port–Cwmmawr). *N.S. Carey*

Empty stock for four return Football Specials to the Valleys, each to be hauled by an ex-GWR '56XX' class 0–6–2T, awaiting calling forward to Ninian Park station on 24th September, 1960. From left to right are No. 5678 on train 2Z30, No. 5663 on 2Z31, 5688 on 2Z34 and 6652 on 2Z32 (to Aberdare). *J. Hodge*

A 'Castle'-hauled up passenger train on the South Wales Main Line between Ely and Cardiff General stations, passing beneath the bridge carrying the PHDR line, in the early 1960s. The bridge carrying the PHDR line has since been rebuilt, in 1968.
A.F. Smith, Peter Rowe (Printers), Cardiff

The 9.55 am Paddington to Swansea train, diverted via the Vale of Glamorgan route to Bridgend, joining the PHDR line at Penarth Curve South Junction on Sunday, 26th January, 1958. The TVR signal box is on the left. The train is hauled by 'Castle' class 4–6–0 No. 5016 *Montgomery Castle.* *R.O. Tuck*

GWR-style 0–6–0PT No. 8466 hauling a freight train from Creigiau off the 'Llantrisant No. 1 Railway' over Waterhall Junction on 18th March, 1964. The layout at Waterhall had been simplified by this date, necessitating this train proceeding to Radyr by being propelled 'wrong road' over the down line. The Creigiau–Waterhall section of line was to close later in 1964, the remaining limestone traffic from Creigiau being routed thenceforward over the Common Branch Junction end of the line until this, too, closed in 1981. *N.S. Carey*

Ex-Barry Railway (nearer the camera) and ex-Rhymney Railway coaches in the sidings at Penarth Town on 12th September, 1958, numbered W274W and W1176W respectively. *R.O. Tuck*

An empty milk train returning to West Wales, diverted via the Vale of Glamorgan because of engineering work on the main line, joining the Barry line at Cogan Junction on Sunday, 18th November, 1962, hauled by ex-GWR 'County' class 4–6–0 No. 1001 *County of Bucks*. To the right, alongside the Penarth line, is the GWR Cogan Junction signal box, and, in the background, the former TVR box. *R.O. Tuck*

A three-car diesel multiple unit train in the process of shunting at Penarth Town for its return working, in the early days of diesel operation, on 17th February, 1958. The train is alongside the site of the former excursion platform. *R.O. Tuck*

Photographed through the cab of a Cardiff-bound dmu, a ballast train stands in the down loop at Cogan Junction on 28th April, 1971 behind class '22' diesel hydraulic locomotive D6327. The up loop is on the left. *D.J. Morgan*

Class '14' diesel hydraulic 0–6–0 locomotive D9547 propelling wagons into Ely Paper Mills on 30th December, 1966. *N.S. Carey*

dard five coach non-corridor suburban trains, each train comprising Brake Third + Third + Compo. + Third + Brake Third.

Numerous such sets were constructed for the valleys, and the Taff trains were gradually broken down into single units. While a few of the carriages were sent elsewhere on the GWR system, mainly as workmen's coaches, and a few others were scrapped, the vast majority of the more modern ex-TVR carriages were retained in the Cardiff Valleys Division and used for workmen. One such carriage was attached to the five-coach sets mentioned above, and detached when not required.

That was still the pattern in the mid-1950s, when workmen's carriages themselves began to disappear from trains. The GWR sets continued in regular use until displaced by three-car diesel suburban sets – augmented to six cars as necessary during peak periods – mainly in 1958 and 1959, and the old steam train carriages gradually faded from the local railway scene. The first regular diesel workings commenced on 13th January, 1958, the three-car sets in question later being known as class 116.

There is no doubt that the passenger service to Penarth Town had changed very little from Grouping until dieselisation. The Taff 0–6–2Ts had been partially replaced by GWR, and occasionally Rhymney, 0–6–2Ts, and finally by 2–6–2Ts, but without any drastic change. Similarly the Taff bogie stock had been replaced by very similar GWR stock. The auto-trains had continued to run in their two-car or four-car formations, even if the Taff overhead gear had been replaced by the GWR system. It is doubtful if the commuters noticed the change, and there were few enthusiasts to do so in the area in those days. The principal post-Grouping changes in both locomotive and rolling stock had been on the Penarth Curve to Cogan section, but that was in connection with the Barry workings already mentioned, and did not affect the line to Penarth Town. In fact, apart from the brief period when the 'Ports to Ports' express was routed via Penarth, it is safe to say that the sight of a tender engine would have caused utter astonishment to the platform staff at Penarth Town. The latter place maintained a very healthy passenger traffic between the wars, during which time its season ticket sales actually rose some 33 per cent.

However things changed rapidly with the end of steam in South Wales in the Summer of 1965, and the closure of Penarth Goods Station as from 4th April, 1966. After that it was a distinct rarity to see anything other than a three-car class 116 diesel suburban set at Penarth Town station, apart from the single car 'Bubble' unit, that continued to ply on the Penarth to Cadoxton section, until that was also closed as from 6th May, 1968.

The latest generation of diesel suburban trains made its debut on the Penarth line on 2nd November, 1985, when prototype 'Sprinter' three-car unit 150001 operated a scheduled service to and from Penarth (15.08 ex-Rhymney, returning at 16.22 from Penarth to Coryton) as part of a visit to the Valley Lines system prior to the opening of Lisvane and Thornhill station (on the ex-Rhymney Railway section) two days later.

The two-car class 150/2 'Sprinter' units which now operate most Valley Lines services, including those to and from Penarth, and those to and from

A dmu-formed railtour train on the Ely Tidal Harbour line, just short of the harbour itself, on 11th July, 1959, one century and one week after the line was opened. The houses of Penarth can be seen in the distance, across the river Ely. The Penarth Railway Hotel, now bereft of its adjacent railway, currently (1992) trades as The Red House. *R.O. Tuck*

The Monmouthshire Railway Society railtour train of April 1987, formed of two class '117', three-car dmu sets, stands outside the Ferry Road BP Oil Terminal, then, as now, the farthest point of the former Ely Tidal Harbour line. Tank cars can be seen in the terminal beyond the train. *D.J. Morgan*

The first refurbished class '116' three-car dmu train to visit Penarth is shown to Councillor Arthur Sanders, Town Mayor, in March 1976. With him (*left to right*) are David Warne, BR Area Manager, Cardiff, Conductor-Guard P. Bennett and Driver F. Cook. In addition to new colour schemes, inside and out, the refurbishing included flourescent lighting and technical improvements to exhaust silencers, fandrive shafts and heater controls. *Courtesy The Penarth Times*

Empty stock of a Royal Train into Cardiff in the process of turning on the Penarth Curves triangle, running onto the Penarth line to reverse at the signal controlling movements off the line. The train is going away from the camera, has passed over Cogan Junction and is now passing the former Penarth Dock station (buildings, *right*). The date is 2nd October, 1984. The leading locomotive (farther from camera) is No. 47500 *Great Western* with No. 47618 at the rear. *R.W. Ranson*

A three-car class '116' diesel multiple unit in blue and grey livery working the 18.17 Penarth to Rhymney service, crossing the Windsor Road bridge on the descent from Dingle Road to Cogan Junction, seen across the roofscape of Cogan on 12th April, 1983. *T.A. Clift*

A railtour train *en route* from Cardiff to Taffs Well and Nantgarw arriving at Radyr off the PHDR line on 28th February, 1987, hauled by two class '33' diesel-electric locomotives, Nos. 33 062 and 33 025, with a class '37', No. 37 905, at the rear. The TVR main line to Cardiff via Llandaff is to the left. *R.W. Ranson*

Barry Island which traverse the PHDR route between Penarth Curve South Junction and Cogan Junction, first entered service on these routes on 7th September, 1987.

However, until the new timetable with its more frequent train service based on two-car operation began on 5th October, 1987 (and operated experimentally on the previous day, Sunday 4th October), some of the new units were temporarily re-formed as three-car units, to replicate the carrying capacity of the three-car class 116 units which they were replacing.

As described in the previous chapter, 5th October, 1987 also saw the opening of a regular passenger service and intermediate stations on the northern section of the PHDR line between Radyr and Ninian Park, the trains continuing via Penarth Curve North and East Junctions to and from Cardiff Central and, mostly, to and from Coryton, the throughout Radyr–Coryton route becoming known as the 'City Line'.

For the first two years the City Line service was operated by Class 150/2 'Sprinters', with the trains generally continuing beyond Radyr to and from Taffs Well or Merthyr Tydfil.

Since October 1989, however, the City Line service throughout most of Weekdays has operated as a self-contained Radyr–Cardiff–Coryton service worked, because of the relatively short distances involved, by the 'first-generation' diesel units, mainly the well-established class 116 – but in two-car formations. Other types, such as the class 108s, were to be seen for a while. As from May 1991 some of the Mondays to Fridays off-peak City Line workings became integrated with the Cardiff–Caerphilly 'shuttles', bringing a few 'Sprinter' units to the middle-day service.

On Weekday evenings the City Line service is regularly operated by 'Sprinters' going through to and from Merthyr Tydfil, as also happens on Sundays when the Aberdare and Merthyr Tydfil trains are routed over the PHDR line to and from Cardiff to provide a service at City Line stations. Indeed, on Summer Sundays since 1991 these Aberdare and Merthyr Tydfil trains have been extended to and from Penarth, reversing at Cardiff Central, providing a rare opportunity of being able to travel over all the passenger-operated sections of the PHDR and Penarth Extension Railway without changing trains!

Since May 1989 a Sunday service between Cardiff and Penarth has operated only during the Summer timetable periods.

Until recently a residue of the early diesel sets, again mainly the class 116 in two-car formation, has also worked over the Penarth and Barry lines on certain peak or Saturday services, but since November 1991 these units have gradually been replaced by the 1985/6-built two-car class 143 'Pacer' diesel multiple unit sets, replete in latest Regional Railways livery, and transferred from Tyneside. In replacing the class 116's, these units, with their four-wheeled cars (but with a modern suspension system) have also become the staple units for the City Line services over the northern section of the PHDR and they also perform numerous workings throughout the Valley Lines system, including regular trips to and from Penarth – and Barry – alongside the larger 'Sprinter' units.

An InterCity 125 forming the 10.15 Paddington to Port Talbot train on Sunday, 13th February, 1983, diverted via Barry and the Vale of Glamorgan line, traversing Cogan Junction. The leading power car and coaches have passed onto the ex-Barry Railway line, with the single track Penarth line nearer the camera. In the right background can be seen the line towards Cardiff with the up and down loops forming a four-track section. *T.A. Clift*

The 15.27 Cardiff Central to Penarth train, formed of two-car 'Sprinter' dmu No. 150230 entering Dingle Road station on 19th August, 1991. *N.W. Sprinks*

Two preserved steam locomotives join the Penarth line at Cogan Junction on Saturday, 6th July, 1985, after working into Cardiff Central on a special train in connection with the 'GWR 150' celebrations. The locomotives are ex-GWR 'Hall' class 4–6–0 No. 4930 *Hagley Hall* and BR-built (GWR design) 'Castle' class 4–6–0 No. 7029 *Clun Castle*. They are in the process of reversing on the Penarth Curves triangular layout, and will reverse on the Penarth line, and again at Penarth Curve North Junction (Ninian Park). *R.W. Ranson*

The 15.15 Radyr–Coryton 'City Line' train arriving at Danescourt on 28th August, 1991, formed of two-car class '116' dmu set C392. *N.W. Sprinks*

The junction at Grangetown, photographed on 15th November, 1990, with the disused (and truncated) line towards Ely Tidal Harbour straight ahead, and the route to Cogan Junction and Penarth veering to the right. The two-car 'Sprinter' unit leaving is the 10.10 Rhymney to Penarth service. This photograph makes an interesting comparison with the lower picture on *page 6*. *N.W. Sprinks*

Two-car class '116' dmu set C391 forming the 14.45 Radyr–Coryton service at Fairwater station on 28th August, 1991. *N.W. Sprinks*

This is the final change in train working to be recorded, although it was not until the weekend of 26th/27th September, 1992, that the last serviceable examples of the valiant, long-lived diesel multiple unit sets from the late 1950s/early 1960s finally left the South Wales scene.

So far as freight operation over the Radyr–Penarth Curves–Cogan Junction sections of the PHDR is concerned, the early diesel age from the 1960s saw a wide variety of diesel traction, including classes '14', '25', '35' ('Hymek'), '43' ('Warship'), '45', '46', '47' and '52' ('Western'). Later scaling down of the diversity of the diesel locomotive fleet into a few standard types has led to the 1,750 hp class '37' now being pre-dominant, with class '47s' appearing on some trains, such as those of tank cars to and from the Barry line.

The frequent 'merry-go-round' trains conveying South Wales coal to Aberthaw power station, which traverse the PHDR either throughout from Radyr to Cogan Junction, or join it only over the Penarth Curve South to Cogan Junctions section, are currently in the hands of class '37s', the usual load being 28 wagons, or some 900 tons payload. This formation has proved more cost-effective than the previous arrangement of double-headed class '37s' with 35 wagons: while in the 1970s class '47s' had been used.

Until they ceased, workings on the Ely Tidal Harbour line (also known in recent years as the Ferry Road branch) were latterly worked by the class '08' 0–6–0 diesel shunters, under special instructions requiring trains to proceed 'cautiously', under supervision of the shunter, and no faster than 8 mph. An official notice dated May 1984, identifies class '08' turn C77 from Canton being available as required on Mondays to Fridays between 07.10 and 11.15 to shunt Canton sidings, the Ferry Road branch, and Virgil Street coal depot – the last named having been alongside the Penarth Curves North to South Junctions line.

The short lived class '14' 0–6–0 diesel freight locomotives worked the Penarth Cement Works trains for a while prior to this traffic ceasing in November 1969, although even here the class '37' latterly took over.

InterCity 125 sets are occasionally seen between Penarth Curve South and Cogan Junctions on London–Swansea workings when the main line between Cardiff and Bridgend is blocked, usually for scheduled engineering works, and the trains are therefore diverted via Barry and the Vale of Glamorgan line. This arrangement usefully preserves 'route knowledge' of the Vale of Glamorgan line for InterCity crews which can be useful at times of emergency diversions. In addition, it is not unknown for an InterCity 125 set requiring turning at Cardiff to do so over the triangle of lines between the three Penarth Curve Junctions. On the Penarth Curve South reversal this has involved the train continuing through Grangetown and Cogan Junction onto the Penarth branch, and reversing at the signal which controls train movements off the branch.

As if to turn the full circle, steam traction made a brief return to the PHDR and PER lines in 1991 as part of the celebrations marking the 150th anniversary of the opening of the TVR's Merthyr Tydfil–Cardiff main line.

On 19th June, three days prior to an Open Day at the ex-TVR Cathays Works, privately owned, preserved, GWR-style 0–6–0PT No. 9466, which

The 10.53 'TVR 150' steam special from Cardiff Central to Aberdare on Sunday, 27th October, 1991 passing Danescourt behind preserved BR standard 2–6–4T No. 80080. Hidden by the exhaust are five Network South East coaches. *R.W. Ranson*

Two-car 'Pacer' dmu No. 143614 at Penarth on 15th April, 1992, after arriving as the 17.55 Cardiff (Bute Road)–Penarth service, and before returning as the 18.21 service to Cardiff Central. *N.W. Sprinks*

The 10.46 Radyr–Coryton 'City Line' train leaving Waun-gron Park station on 27th November, 1991, formed of two-car 'Pacer' diesel multiple unit No. 143601, then recently transferred from Tyneside for use in South Wales. *N.W. Sprinks*

Two-car 'Pacer' dmu No. 143609 at Fairwater on 8th April, 1992, forming the 11.16 Radyr–Coryton train. *N.W. Sprinks*

Preserved GWR-style 0–6–0PT No. 9466 standing close to the TVR Radyr Quarry signal box during a 'photo-call' on 19th June, 1991 to help publicise the Taff Vale Railway 150th anniversary celebrations. The locomotive was built in BR days (1951) and was at one time shedded at Radyr.

G. Johns

was built for BR Western Region in 1951 and was at one time allocated to Radyr shed, performed a steam shunting 'photo call' in Radyr yard and at the erstwhile 'Penarth Junction'.

Then in September and October, special steam hauled passenger trains were operated over the Valley Lines using the privately owned BR Standard 2–6–4T No. 80080 (built at Brighton in 1954). Of the 22 trips performed by this locomotive, the first trial light-engine trip from Canton depot to Merthyr Tydfil in the early hours of Sunday, 29th September, ran via Ninian Park and the PHDR route to Radyr. On Sunday morning, 6th October, No. 80080 took a special passenger train from Cardiff Central to Barry and back, traversing the PHDR in both directions between Penarth Curve South and Cogan Junctions.

But the PHDR and PER came into their own on the final day of steam specials, Sunday, 27th October. No. 80080 worked a 10.10 special from Cardiff Central to Penarth, returning at 10.26. Diesel No. 37 699 was attached at the rear on leaving Cardiff to haul the train back from Penarth in the absence now of run-round facilities at the end of the branch. On arrival at Cardiff Central No. 80080 and the train formed the 10.53 special to Aberdare, which was the only passenger carrying special in the steam programme to run via Penarth Curve East and North Junctions and the PHDR route, to reach the 'Taff' main line at Radyr.

These days provided a very different spectacle from the normal routine of modern diesel trains, but an enjoyable interlude, and an historic and interesting note on which to conclude this book.

Appendix One

Route Mileage

		As constructed		*Still open*	
		M.	*Ch.*	*M.*	*Ch.*
PHDR	Penarth Jn (Radyr) to Grangetown Jn	4	46	OPEN	
	Grangetown Jn to termination of Harbour Branch.	1	46	Approx. 62 ch. IN SITU OUT OF USE	
	Grangetown Jn to Penarth Dock Branch Jn	1	31	OPEN	
	Penarth Dock Branch Jn – terminus of dock (north side).	0	70	CLOSED	
	Penarth Dock Branch Jn – terminus of dock (south side).	0	70	CLOSED	
PER	Penarth Dock Branch Jn – Penarth Town Stn.	1	15	OPEN	
CPBJR	Penarth Town Stn – Biglis Jn (Cadoxton)	4	55	CLOSED	

Running Powers Biglis Jn – Cadoxton Station (Barry Ry) OM 32C

Appendix Two

Stations, Rail Car Platforms, Junctions, etc.

	Mileage from Radyr Junction m. ch.	*Station Opened*	*Station Closed*	*Remarks*
Radyr Quarry Junction	0 39			
DANESCOURT	1 21	5.10.1987†	—	
Waterhall Junction	1 51			Goods Yard closed 13.7.1964. Branch closed 28.9.1964
FAIRWATER/TYLLGOED	1 61	5.10.1987†	—	
Ely Goods Yard	2 07			Renamed 'Ely Fairwater Road' 1.7.1924. Closed 1.7.1963.
WAUN-GRON PARK	2 16	2.11.1987	—	
Ely Paper Mills (Ground Frame)	2 63			
Leckwith Junction	3 52			
*NINIAN PARK	3 58	2.11.1912	—	Rebuilt and second platform added 1932/3: regular passenger train service introduced 5.10.1987†.
Penarth Curve North Junction	3 74			
Penarth Curve South Junction	4 19			
GRANGETOWN	4 45	Autumn 1882	—	Rebuilt as island platform c.1904.
Grangetown Junction	4 46			
*LLANDOUGH	5 62	13.6.1904	1.6.1918	
Penarth Dock Branch Junction	5 77			
Cogan Junction	6 01			
PENARTH DOCK	6 13	20.2.1878	1.1.1962	
*DINGLE ROAD	6 57	1.3.1904	—	
PENARTH (TOWN)	7 09	20.2.1878	—	Second platform added 15.4.1889. Closed for goods traffic 4.4.1966. End of line now at 7 m 12 ch.
*ALBERTA PLACE	7 41	19.9.1904	6.5.1968	
LOWER PENARTH	8 07	1.2.1897	14.6.1954	
Penarth Cement Works	8 52			Closed 11.1969
LAVERNOCK	8 79	1.12.1887	6.5.1968	Closed for goods traffic 7.10.1963.
*SWANBRIDGE	9 67	6.1906	6.5.1968	
SULLY	10 63	24.12.1888	6.5.1968	Open for goods traffic 5.11.1888 to 7.10.1963. Temporary passenger station at c.11 m 63 ch 8.7.1889 to 22.5.1890.
Biglis Junction	11 67			

*Opened as Rail Car Platforms by the TVR.